More praise for GIRLS ON TRACK

"*Girls on Track* is a wonderful strategy for girls to get through their adolescence with their sense of self intact and pride blossoming. It provides clear guidelines for adults and girls to incorporate healthy empowering into their lives."
—ROSALIND WISEMAN, Author of *Queen Bees and Wannabes*

"If you believe in possibilities still undreamed . . . if you believe in change not yet manifest . . . if you believe in young girls out there and the young girl deep inside each grown woman, then believe in this book. Molly Barker's story has the power to change you, your life, and the lives of everyone you love."
—DANNYE ROMINE POWELL
Author of *Parting the Curtains: Interviews with Southern Writers*

"Very inspiring. Great message. A wonderful book for moms looking to connect/reconnect with their daughters. Provides great insight into the struggles that girls face in today's society. The author provides the reader with a step-by-step guide on how to reach out and mentor a child to be all that they can be."
—NANCY LIEBERMAN
Former WNBA player and coach, ESPN commentator

"Molly Barker's personal battle with the Girl Box somehow gave rise to a truly remarkable program. I wish every young girl could experience Girls on the Run and *Girls on Track*."
—RUSSELL R. PATE, Ph. D., Professor and Associate Dean for Research Arnold School of Public Health, University of South Carolina

"Molly Barker's personal journey, chronicled in *Girls on Track*, is not simply inspirational, but heroic. recognizing that girls are so often limited by what is expected of them in terms of appearance, personality, intelligence, and achievement, Molly has given us all a plan so that we can climb out of the Girl Box and make sure our daughters don't climb into the box at all. Molly's message? It is just fine if our daughters are dirty, sweaty, and have a voice. Run, Molly, run."
—MARY MAZZIO, Award-winning filmmaker and former Olympian

GIRLS
ON
TRACK

A Parent's Guide to Inspiring
Our Daughters to Achieve a Lifetime
of Self-Esteem and Respect

MOLLY BARKER

BALLANTINE BOOKS • NEW YORK

A Ballantine Book
Published by The Random House Publishing Group
Copyright © 2004 by Molly Barker

www.ballantinebooks.com

Library of Congress Cataloging-in-Publication Data

Barker, Molly.
Girls on track / Molly Barker.— 1st ed.
p.   cm.
1. Girls—Psychology.   2. Preteens—Psychology.   3. Self-acceptance.
4. Barker, Molly.—Childhood and youth.   I. Title.

HQ777.B26 2004
155.5'33—dc22   2003045138

ISBN 0-345-45686-6

Book design by Susan Turner

Manufactured in the United States of America

First Edition: April 2004

1   3   5   7   9   10   8   6   4   2

CONTENTS

INTRODUCTION
1

ONE
MY BELLY BUTTON AND
THE TERRITORY AROUND IT 13

TWO
A LIFE IN TRAINING 40

THREE
SHE'S IN THERE 51

FOUR
IN THE CARDS 84

FIVE
MAKING THE MOST OF YOUR
CLIMBING-OUT-OF-THE–GIRL BOX EXPERIENCE 107

SIX
GETTING READY FOR YOUR FIRST 5K 224

SEVEN
WHEN MOTHERS RULE THE WORLD 233

EPILOGUE
242

ACKNOWLEDGMENTS
245

INTRODUCTION

In 1976, I bought my first pair of running shoes.

I was fifteen then and, like most fifteen-year-old girls, trying to figure out who I was inside a changing body. I desperately wanted to be liked by the beautiful crowd, to be popular with the boys. But I couldn't quite fit into the Girl Box the world wanted to place over the spark of my spirit.

The Girl Box told me things I knew in my soul weren't true. That the way I looked was more important than who I was inside. That being a woman meant keeping emotions like anger to myself. That having a boyfriend was worth giving up part of my own identity. But I stepped into the box anyway. I spent hours trying to mold my body, my lifestyle, my life into what the box required. Those hours were extremely painful.

So I ran. I'd strap on those running shoes and head for the woods, the streets, wherever my feet would take me. I felt beautiful, strong, powerful. When I ran, I felt a part of something greater than myself.

Yet despite the running, I compromised myself. I lost Molly somewhere in the box, eight feet down in the brown darkness of materialism, external desires, and appearance. The wonderful, unique, and wild little girl that made me *me* was frightened and hiding.

Then on July 7, 1993, I put on my running shoes, as usual, and ran at sunset. I'm not sure in what moment during the run the box disappeared, but like a glass womb it shattered around me and pushed me out, born to an entirely new freedom. It was a moment of personal awakening. A year later I began work on what was to become the Girls on the Run program.

What Is the Girl Box?

I coined the term *Girl Box* to describe the dark place that girls—previously happy, confident girls—reluctantly go into about the time of fifth grade, often with heartbreaking results. The girl who knew all the answers becomes the girl who hides in the back of the class; the girl who could beat the boys at races becomes the girl who feels ashamed of her strong body and legs; the girl who giggled with her friends becomes the girl who is silent and afraid.

Before I started Girls on the Run International, I worked as a teacher, social worker, counselor, and coach, and I watched many girls go through negative changes starting at this critical age. I would watch formerly confident, self-assured girls take on a more depressed posture, defer to boys in the classroom, be flirty instead of smart, complain of weight problems where there were none, or feel left out because they couldn't afford the "right" outfit. Not coincidentally, psychologists believe fifth grade is around the same time that a large number of severe mental disorders begin to crop up: substance abuse, eating disorders, early sexual contact, depression, and the "disorder" that seems to affect most women with whom I come into contact: "people pleasing."

Through my own experiences and those of others, I realized that in the Girl Box, women suddenly *perform* their lives, as opposed to experiencing them. Down in the darkness of the Girl Box, they lose their spirit and morph into whatever they believe society wants them to be: what they see in magazines; what they see on television; what they see in their own families. I know this all too well, as I, too, am a former inhabitant of the Girl Box.

What Is Girls on the Run International?

In 1996, after years of personal struggle and professional training, I started Girls on the Run. After that fated July run three years earlier, I knew I had to do two things: take every opportunity I could to live outside of the Girl Box and inspire young girls to do the same. One of the main precepts of the program is that participating in sports provides essential tools for girls to weather the turbulent years of teenhood—and adulthood as well. There is much research and evidence to back this up, as we'll discuss.

Girls on the Run is therefore an experiential learning program that combines training girls in grades three to eight for a 3.1-mile running event with games and life lessons that assist in their physical, emotional, mental, social, and *spiritual* development. Our mission? **To educate and prepare girls for a lifetime of self-respect and healthy living.** We address the individual girl's identity and personal connections with others, as well as her potential feeling of powerlessness within herself and her community. Participants in Girls on the Run explore the importance of being physically, mentally, and emotionally healthy. They examine their own core values and uniqueness. And they also examine body-image issues, stereotyping, and discriminatory behaviors, as well as the importance of maintaining a realistic and healthy view of themselves. Girls take from the program a better understanding of how to process the cultural and social messages they receive through media and other institutions. And they see a stronger place for themselves within their community.

Take Delila, for example. The story of Delila is perhaps an extreme one, for Delila has known more pain in her short life than many of us will ever know. But her story shows us how Girls on the Run can help girls—even girls in situations of extreme difficulty—find their voices and climb out of the Girl Box.

Delila was in fourth grade when I met her. She had recently been adopted. Delila has known darkness, more darkness than you would wish upon even your very worst enemy. She has scars the size of cigarette butts across her back and thighs to show for it. She runs from a camera, uncertain of what unseemly pose the photographer will require of her. She has problems with her eyesight from sitting in darkness for long periods of time. And Delila doesn't talk. It's not that she doesn't know how—it's that she *won't* talk. Talking, where she came from, only got you in trouble. Using your voice and speaking up for yourself—expressing your fears, your emotions—only got you scars, darkness, or worse: nothing. Delila joined Girls on the Run after her adoptive parents encouraged her to do so.

I had the privilege of being her coach. Typically in most of our games we have a processing period after each game or activity—an opportunity for the girls to relate the experience of the game to some real-life situation. Going around our circle of seventeen, I would come to Delila. Each day, Delila would nervously shake her head and look to the ground, and we would move on to the next girl in the circle. The first week, one of the other girls said fondly "Oh, that's just Delila, she never talks." As the weeks went on, Delila kept coming back and she kept shaking her head when given the opportunity to speak.

But girl, could Delila run. She communicated her moods, her feelings, her thoughts by how her body moved through space. When she was mad, her feet would slam the pavement, her stride choppy. Her blond hair would sporadically rise and fall with each step. But when she was right with the world, for that one hour of her life, she would float across the asphalt, each step tapping the pavement, ever so lightly, her arms relaxed at her side and her blond hair flowing in a stream behind her.

On the very last workout day of that session of Girls on the Run I asked the girls to name one or two words that would describe their Girls on the Run experience. Katherine said, "Cool!" Anna said, "Awesome." Takia said, "The bomb." (That means great!) And Delila . . . she paused, cleared her throat, and said . . . nothing. She shook her head and looked to the ground, and we continued. The following night we had our Girls on the Run banquet. Each participant receives her very own award, based on what makes her special. Katherine won the Smile with the Red Face award. Anna won the Loyal to Her Friends award. Takia won the Cool Cat award.

And Delila, what award did she win? Delila won the Grand Communicator award—for communicating on a level that surpasses anything worldly. She could communicate with her body, the strike of her step, the look in her eye, the smile on her face.

When I called Delila up to receive her award—she slowly moved to take her place next to me. And out of her back pocket she pulled out a small card. With a nod of her head she handed it to me and I opened it. As I opened it and read it, her face lit up, knowing that today was special, today something different would happen. Today, Delila would find her voice. I asked her if she would like to read what she wrote—and that brave little girl closed her eyes tight, so tight, for a few seconds, dug deep, and read her very own words to all of her friends in Girls on the Run and their families. Oh, the sound of her sweet voice, like music through the room. "The word I wanted to say on the last day of Girls on the Run was *love*."

Delila got her voice back that day. Somewhere it had been lost—or taken from her—in the darkness of some unknown closet, a burn, or a photo. But on this day, Delila took it back. And I along with her friends had the privilege to witness her courage, her fear, and her *right* to use her voice in whatever way she chose and with whatever words she wanted. The girl had been released! Epiphany.

I ran into Delila recently. She is now a budding teenager. School was out for a teachers' workday and she was bouncing into the Y with her best friend. A smile stretched from here to California when she saw me. I asked her if I could give her a hug and she shook her head no, making very little eye contact with me. But when I asked her how she was doing, she said, "Good," in that young teenage way, as in, "Good—what else did you expect me to say?" I asked her where she was in school. She told me. I asked her if she was running and she said yes. Delila had a voice and was using it. The grin that went along with it made it more beautiful than I remembered. As I walked away from her she gave me a little punch on my arm and said, "Thanks for asking."

The encounter was brief, but one I needed on that day— one that I needed at this incredible time of global mistrust, fear, and uncertainty. That encounter reminded me that what Girls on the Run is doing is so important, so critical in our world. Little girls and big girls need their voices. They need to feel free to express who they are—all of their fears, their frustrations, their *anger*—so that they can communicate their complete and perfect spirit to the world. Delila's story is the perfect example of how we can overcome trauma, distrust, and hatred with self-expression, emotion, and love.

There are countless stories like Delila's that come from Girls on the Run chapters throughout the United States. The program reaches girls from all socioeconomic groups, ethnic groups, and geographical regions. Girls who are already strong and healthy enroll in the program to further strengthen and enhance their self-esteem. Girls whose self-esteem needs a boost also enroll in the program. Girls on the Run is unique in that it offers a unified voice and a unified experience for ALL girls—regardless of income or level of esteem.

Why the Book and Not Just the Program?

What humbly started with thirteen girls in Charlotte, North Carolina, in 1996 now boasts thousands of girls in eighty-six cities and forty-one states. Every day we get phone calls. Phone calls from moms just like me. Phone calls from dads who want to do the right thing and from educators who want to try something different. All of them want to DO something, do *anything* to encourage and celebrate the goodness of the girls they work with, play with, or live with. They want to do whatever they can to strengthen their little girls so that they become strong, healthy women.

They call me because they've heard that Girls on the Run can help them.

I remember, way back when the Girls on the Run concept first began to take shape in my thoughts, I had this vision of running around the track with a dozen little girls running beside me. A little *Rocky*-ish, I admit, but the image was strong, powerful and it led me to believe that I might be able to one day lead those little girls over, around, and out of the Girl Box— out of the negative stereotypes and messages they get through the media, culturally, and socially.

But as I soon learned, if I ran during the games and the workouts, I was able to run with only a few girls who kept the same pace as I did. This limited my interaction to those few who ran alongside me. The others, who ran at their own pace, didn't really share the experience with me. So after that first meeting, I realized the importance of staying put in one position on the track and letting those little girls run *by* me. "Way to go, Katherine." "Good job, Delila." I could high-five each girl, look her in the eye, acknowledge her job well done, and— for the instant that we occupied the same space on the track— focus all my attention on her.

Although Girls on the Run operates chapters all across the United States and Canada, what many mothers, fathers, and educators want is impossible to provide in large groups: a one-on-one experience, a completely uninterrupted space in time when two people—a girl and someone who loves her—can share and explore their thoughts and feelings around the Girl Box and the messages they get from it.

This book is intended to help you establish this one-on-one experience. It takes the lessons and precepts of Girls on the Run and translates them into a program for individual girls and the grown-ups who love them and want to see them break out of the dreaded box. The book may be used in conjunction with the program or on its own.

My little girl is growing up so fast. While I'm trying to be the best example of a woman joyously living outside of the Girl Box, she is still bombarded by messages and seductive promises that entice her into the box. She and I will definitely do this set of lessons together—over and over. Truthfully, I need them at least as much as she does—and like any good book its message mysteriously changes over time as we mature and our life circumstances change. Each time you read this book and each time you go through the lessons with your daughter, she will be a little more grown-up—and you will be a little wiser.

Yes, my little Helen is growing up. She is now four years old. She doesn't come into my room in the middle of the night as much as she used to. She holds tight to her own sheets, enjoys the independence of knowing that she slept the entire night in her own bed. Surrounded by the comfort of her teddy bear, her Barbies—some naked, some painted on, some clad in the latest Barbie style—she is peaceful in her own space, clutching that teddy bear tight.

Like Helen, Girls on the Run—the very concept upon which this book is based—is also growing up, seeking the independence of its own bed, not so enmeshed with me that making it through the night is a scary prospect. How wonderful that it can cling tightly to its own sheets.

I'm okay with Helen's independence. I know, in my heart, that it is good for her to no longer need my body warmth to embrace her—to comfort her through the night. But I do miss the intimacy of it. I miss that early-morning snuggle—the coming in when the sky has a hint of pink, or white, or orange, depending on the emerging day. I miss her little-girl smell, the softness of her skin, and the thick little arms and legs that would rest lightly—even in their thickness—across my abdomen as she wrapped her strong, feminine body about me. I miss the warmth of her small body, listening to her breathing—tiny puffs of air that lift her still-round belly up and down—gently hearing that through the night silence. I miss her . . .

Although Helen may be growing up and may not need me as she once did, I need her and I can choose to go to her bed and snuggle with her. I can feel the warmth of her all over again, remember what it felt like: celebrate her independence and know that it is essential to her health.

This book is like that for me. It gives me the chance to remember Girls on the Run in its infancy, the reason I started it, the joy of discovering pieces of myself that I didn't know were there—the celebration of myself, my own daughter, and the work that I do.

Over the holidays, Helen lifted a plaster handprint I made when I was around her age from the ornament box. MOLLY 1963 is inscribed in the white stone. She placed her delicate hand in the print—her small fingers over my tiny girl print. "Mommy, is this mine?"

It's hard now that I'm an adult to hold back some of the melancholy of remembering my own youth—the reflection, sorrow in some ways, and this overwhelming feeling that life is going by so quickly.

The feel of that white plaster in my hands. Smooth and sturdy, the lines of my four-year-old fingerprints delicately raised in the drying of it. The tiny Molly—the little spirit that patiently rested her hand in that wet plaster—who waited to let it mold around her hand. The little red ribbon threaded through a small hole at the top—to be hung on each holiday tree since then.

That small plaster ornament has been on each and every holiday tree of my life, since its creation. Families changing, parents divorcing, parents dying, new houses, boyfriends, my growing up, marriages, children being born, marriages ending, yet always that seasonal reminder of who I was.

Throughout my life my Higher Power has given me plaster—

mixed with years of pain, shame, experience, growth, forgiveness, acceptance, amends, and love.

And as I write this book, my Higher Power gives me the
courage to put my handprint on that plaster and name it *Girls
on Track*.

Over the years, this book will see many changes. Children
being born, girls growing up, girls crying, laughing, celebrating,
learning, and exploring—it will see many changes in our own
adult lives, our aging, our growing, our dying.

I believe, as much as I believe anything, that we are on the
edge of a shift so great, so powerful, so far-reaching, so *real* that
we can't even begin to imagine it. None of this would be possible without the amazing people like you, who take the time to
spend with a girl—to play with her, nurture her, and love her
from the deepest part of yourself.

And so at this time in my precious life—you reading this
book and sharing the ten-week experience with a little girl
whom you love, my daughter clutching her own space, and my
chance, again, to remember what it was like, what happened,
and what it is like now—I can do nothing but consider myself
the most blessed woman in the world—grateful for the gift of
Girls on the Run, the spirit of this book, and the people like
you whom it attracts.

I am blessed by the very spirit of it.

And so when Helen asks each holiday season (because she
always does), "Mommy is this mine?", when she places her
small hand on the white plaster ornament, blessing it with her
innocence and anticipation, I say, "Yes, my girl. It is. It is yours.
It is mine.

"It is ours."

I hope you and your girl enjoy the journey you are about
to trek and that you find the book a helpful guide. I hope it

kick-starts an opportunity for you to celebrate, to grow, and to explore all the complex issues around being a girl in today's society.

And have some fun doing it.

Peace,
Molly Barker

ONE

MY BELLY BUTTON AND
THE TERRITORY AROUND IT

I was in sixth grade when the Girl Box began to wedge its way over my body and spirit. Sixth grade was a tough year. I had started a new school—forced to leave the comfort of familiar friends to attend a private school in Charlotte, North Carolina. I barely got in. I was on the waiting list for a while and didn't know I'd been accepted until a few weeks before school started.

Eleanor Jones was my best friend then. She was new, too. We were the two new girls at a school where most kids had started kindergarten together.

The thing that distinguished us from each other, however, was that Eleanor was getting breasts and I wasn't. We were new, and all of the boys were noticing Eleanor.

That's when I started to want to be somebody else. Anybody but me. My charming personality just wasn't hacking it.

Neither was my intelligence, my humor, or even my athleticism. None of that was working. The boys still wanted to pop Eleanor's bra strap, chase her, and be in *her* company. I happened to be in their company because I was friends with Eleanor. That was the only reason. I felt like the third wheel all the time—even when I wasn't with Eleanor.

Contrast that with the summer before sixth grade. I was ten years old. The Hortons had a huge holly bush in their front yard. That darn bush stood about five feet high and was right next to their wraparound porch. Jamie, a boy in my neighborhood, stood a good two inches shorter than me and weighed five to ten pounds less. He challenged me to fly over that bush— to jump from the porch to the soft grass five feet below. "I'll bet you can't do it, Molly, because after all, you're just a *girl*."

I *could* do it. Being a girl had nothing to do with it. I could do anything. I was a natural athlete—little knobby knees, muscle on bone, ribs showing. I preferred shorts, no shirt, and bare feet over my Sunday best, even on Sunday. That same summer I went to my first overnight camp. I didn't shower all week. My hair, short and boyish, was strawlike from endless hours in the pool. "Eau de chlorine" suited me quite well, thank you.

My hair was usually tucked under a baseball cap. By week's end, when my counselor pulled the cap off, my hair just stayed put. "You'd better wash that hair before your parents get here," she said. I did wash my hair, with soap. A small swarm of insects that had set up shop in that tangled mess of dirt and chlorine flew off my head. I screamed bloody murder as a family of buzzing insects circled out of the shower spray. My friend Susan screamed, too. I fled from the shower buck naked to my counselor's cabin barefoot, over rocks and sticks, bugs buzzing all around my wet, soapy head. She helped scrub them out.

Bugs in my hair. How gross.

Bugs in my hair. How cool.

So being a girl had nothing to do with it. I prepared myself for the flight over the holly bush. I marched right up to that porch, concentrated really hard for a minute—eyes closed tight, nose scrunched, and arms held out at a 90-degree angle while all the neighborhood kids stood there, the suspense building. (I was such a drama queen.) Then, with no warning at all, I began flapping my arms like a huge pterodactyl and started running. I took as many steps as I could and then with wild abandon I leaped off that front porch and clear over that bush.

I crash-landed on the other side. Jamie said I didn't do it right because I didn't land on my feet. It hurt to land on my girl chest. That was the first time I'd ever had the wind totally knocked from me, and I was truly scared. I couldn't breathe. I lay there on my belly for a minute, trying to catch a deep breath and hold back the tears. All the kids rushed over—all except Jamie, who stood alone trying to make his case that a two-footed landing was the only official way to clear the bush.

I felt something inside me. A smile—small at first—but it felt really good creeping through my body. That smile started with the return of my breathing and crept its way through my heart to my face. I rolled over on my back, bounced up. *Hey, I'm okay. I'm standing. I did it.* I felt that smile move to my feet. I danced right there—a small jig—completely joyous and unin- hibited. I had done it!

But in sixth grade the boys weren't interested in what I could do. They didn't want to play the same way they had just the summer before. They wanted to pop bra straps and chase Eleanor around the playground. I didn't understand what I had done wrong. I was still funny, considerate, and friendly. I was bright, witty, and athletic. But I wasn't Eleanor. I wasn't what Eleanor represented.

And so I reluctantly let them lower the Girl Box over me. It was suffocating in there.

I was a prime candidate for the Girl Box. I was the fourth of four, nine years younger than the one before me. My mother was an alcoholic and my father worked a lot. Everyone in my house seemed to want to be somewhere other than where they were. My sister Helen was my primary caregiver. She taught me to read. She took me on dates with her and tried her best to protect me from the chaos of our home.

We used to visit my grandmother a lot. She lived a day's drive away. My grandmother talked to herself all the time. I used to be embarrassed by this strange behavior. I thought it was weird. Today, I might call her a free spirit. But then I was a little bit afraid of her.

On one of those trips, when I was five, my mother, grandmother, sister, and I went to a friend of my grandmother's. Everything in the house smelled old and musty—the burgundy velvet antique chairs and the lime-green paisley print couch. My mother, grandmother, and her friend started drinking. The ice tinkled in their glasses and the woman who owned the house kept pouring the clear liquid. I was scared and can remember secretly wishing inside myself that they wouldn't do that—drink that stuff, I mean. I couldn't name what scared me about it. I clung to Helen.

My mother started laughing too loud. I wanted to fly away. I wanted to go to bed—just be anywhere but there. Be anybody but me. Helen took me in the guest bedroom in this big, musty, smelly house and lay down with me. She wrapped her teenage body around my little-girl spirit and sang to me—trying to drown out the noise of the inappropriate conversation and laughter out in the living room. I think I cried. I can't remember.

The front door of that stinky place slammed shut. Were they leaving or coming back? Was it minutes or hours since we'd gotten there? My sister cracked open the door of the bedroom and peered out into the living room. I stood behind her, trembling—wanting to look but not wanting to look. The older ladies weren't laughing as loud—in fact they weren't laughing at all. My mother had mud on her knees—mud mixed with blood that was dripping down her shins. Mud covered her face like some horrible Halloween mask.

Somewhere she had fallen.

I don't remember how we got back to my grandmother's apartment. I was asleep in a small room. The door opened and my mother came in. I remember the strong smell of Palmolive soap and Scope mouthwash. I pretended I was asleep as she curled up behind me. I don't know how long she lay there with me. Before she left the room, I heard her whisper in the most sorrowful voice I had ever heard, "I'm so sorry, my little Molly." When she left the room and shut that door, I cried myself to sleep.

This kind of memory doesn't go away—even from a five-year-old. So it settled down inside me. There were lots of memories like this.

Our local newspaper was doing a story on an art contest and somehow my well-connected father had gotten me to be the poster child for the contest. I was in second grade. My hair stuck out a lot and I had two huge front teeth growing into spaces left by smaller baby teeth. I wore my Mickey Mouse watch every day and smocks that used to be my sisters'.

Today was the day. But rather than feeling excited about the attention, I was terrified down to my very core. I shook all day, threw up a couple of times, and had diarrhea. What would I find when I came home today? Would my mother be drunk? Would she be "asleep" on the couch, a cigarette burning in the ashtray on the coffee table? Would she smell funny, talk funny, and act funny? *Dear God, please, today of all days, let her be right.*

I don't want them to find out—not the newspaper people. Then the whole world will find out. They will figure out what I want so much to hide. I won't be able to hide the yucky, scary feeling in my belly anymore. They will discover that my mother has something wrong with her and it has to do with the sweet, stinging way her breath smells and the weird way she talks.

Please, dear God, just let her be okay today. Just today. That is all I ask.

I walked home that day by myself. My friend Susan usually walked with me, but today my pace was too quick even for her. I turned the corner and ran down the street to our house. Oh my God, two cars were out front. They were here. They had found her, lying motionless on the couch. *Maybe she's dead and her mouth has that sweet stinky smell coming out of it. I had nothing to do with it, I promise. It's not my fault, really. Or is it?* My heart pounded so hard, I thought it might explode out of my ears.

They took my photograph while I drew a picture of a horse. My mom stood in the adjacent room, smoking a cigarette, watching. I am smiling in the photograph. They combed my hair, straightened my collar, and put a little color on my cheeks. "Molly, you are looking awfully pale today. Are you feeling all right?"

I was just picture-perfect. I had to be or else they would find out.

Somewhere around fourth grade, the memories shut off— the pain went underground. The psyche does some pretty amazing protective things, especially for little girls when the hurt is too great.

It was not until my mother had her breakdown a year later that my memories resumed. Dr. Thomas came to the house, my father came home from work, and they all talked very secretly in the guest bedroom. My mother hit what folks in the treatment world call bottom.

That was May of 1970. I'm happy to say that my mother is now a recovering alcoholic and has been since that day. Our relationship flourished, the laughter returned to our house. We made family trips out West, spent weekends together staying up and snuggling. We made up for lost time. I absolutely loved my mother's company and would opt for it over that of my friends. The blinds had been lifted and, like Dorothy stepping out into the land of Oz, my life was Technicolor, bright and vibrant. My mother had become my best friend.

But inside the pit of my being lay those lost memories, the shame that we never really talked about. And as I grew both physically and chronologically, that shame started to ooze out in all kinds of ways: insecurity, low self-esteem, perfectionism, people pleasing—all of the classic child-of-an-alcoholic symptoms and in many ways the symptoms of someone down deep in the Girl Box.

So when Eleanor started to get all the attention, the world was simply affirming what I had experienced as a younger child. I wasn't good enough. The shame in there was so deeply learned—throughout each and every cell of my little-girl body. Obviously if I had been good enough, my mother would have stopped drinking. I was funny, friendly, and smart . . . but not enough to make my mother happy. If I was a good person, people would like me—so because they didn't and I couldn't make it all right, something was wrong with me. The best that I could be, the best that I could offer, wasn't fixing my scary home, curing my mother's illness, or making people like me.

Something was definitely wrong with me.

So as painful as it was, the box actually felt sort of right. It was the only place that affirmed what I believed to be true and had experienced in my young life. The message of the Girl Box is do more, be more, give more—because you are never good enough, never pretty enough, never smart enough, never sexy enough, never enough. Girls in the darkness of that box never celebrate what they are but are constantly seeking what they are not. They give away their very souls to anyone who will love them. People pleasing becomes a way of life. Life becomes a series of performances rather than experiences. Your words aren't your own. There is a set script.

So in 1975, when I was in tenth grade, that first sip of liquor at a friend's house burned on its way down, but it pierced that shame. For the brief period I was under its influence that shame went away—the alcohol penetrated it like chemo on cancer—and I felt beautiful, flirtatious, witty, fearless. For the first time I felt comfortable in the Girl Box—shameless and free to be something I was not. I could fake the script, play the part, be what the Girl Box wanted me to be.

Everyone has their ways of coping with the Girl Box. It may be an obsession with appearance or a fear of failure. Some fear success, and sabotage every opportunity to get it. Others defer to boys in the classroom or men in the workplace. Some women spend their entire lives trying to please others and forget themselves. We fix people, clean up after others, take care of disputes— we spend so much time taking care of others that we lose ourselves in the process. More extreme coping mechanisms include eating disorders, countless sexual encounters, numerous plastic surgeries, substance abuse, or spending money we don't have— mine was alcohol.

In the midst of this, I bought my first pair of running shoes. My mother had started running: first one time around the block, then a couple of times. By 1976 she was competing in 5K and 10K events throughout the region and winning her fifty-and-over age-group. I decided to join her on some of those runs. And on those runs I transcended all of the expectations of the Girl Box. Outside of drinking, running was the only place where I felt free from the anxiety and shame of my earlier years.

Like meditation, it cleared my mind and allowed me to focus on the sound of my steps, the rhythm of my breathing, and the air passing over my body. I sweated; sometimes I would grunt and groan with exertion and I didn't care that it wasn't feminine. When I ran, I returned to the carefree days of an imaginary fourth grade that I actually never had.

I continued the outer life of the high achiever, the perfect girl/athlete/student. National Honor Society, president of student council, honor society in college, sorority, chemistry major, stellar athlete, nationally ranked triathlete and three-time Ironman Triathlete, high school teacher and coach, masters in social work—the list of accomplishments grew and grew. But nothing—not the working out, not the perfect job, not the right man, nor the right things—could quiet the screaming of that shame. Even running stopped working the more competitive I became. The focus in my training shifted from the experience itself to the end result—the victory: how I placed and who I beat, instead of how good I felt or what I learned about myself. The only thing that would smother the pain was alcohol. But here is the irony of it. While the alcohol could numb that shame for the periods of time that I was under its influence, it was also feeding it: the next morning, the shame would be bigger and louder, vibrating throughout my entire body.

I recently came across a diary that I kept during high school:

July 24, 1976: Sometimes I feel like running away. I am seriously considering it now. I don't think Daddy understands me or Mother for that matter. I'm going out with David tonight. Daddy will probably be angry. I have a terrible feeling of guilt, all the time. I feel as though death or something terrible is right around the corner. I'm scared. Really frightened. I'm growing up too fast. . . . Last night I went to the Elton John concert. I've never been that drunk before. This morning I got sick. After Elton John's concert, David and I went parking. The more I think about it the more worried and frightened I become. I was so drunk he probably could have made love to me and gotten away with it, easily. . . . You know he said things to me I never imagined ever spoken. I believe he really loves me. At least I want to believe he really loves me. . . .

Only one short year after my first taste of alcohol I was having blackouts regularly. (Blackouts are different from passing out. During a blackout, an intoxicated person continues to move about and appears to be functioning yet will have no memory of any events that occur.) On the first occasion I had gone to my best friend's mountain house for New Year's Eve. I was in tenth grade. There were kegs of beer and flowing champagne at midnight. My boyfriend, David, of about a year was there, too. We all were dancing, laughing—there must have been about fifteen of my classmates at her house. Sometime during the night things went from clear to foggy. I ended the evening making out with a different boy, a football player, one of the popular guys—at least until I began to throw up all over my friend's house. I don't remember any of this. My peers considered taking me to the hospital—but rather than let any of the adults know, they took care of my vomiting, dehydration, and convulsions themselves. I'm lucky I didn't die. I came out of a blackout in the backyard of her house with someone putting snow on my face, trying to wash off the vomit.

Now fast-forward ten years to Charleston, South Carolina. I'm sick and blacking out nearly every weekend, although now there was no steady boyfriend, no friend's mountain house—just strangers, mixed drinks, and very little memory. I was teaching at a high school. Teaching was the occupation that best suited me during those years. I seemed to have a way with high school–age kids and while I was struggling with my drinking, which I tried to confine to weekends, I was still pretty much holding it together for my job.

I traveled back to Charlotte frequently during that year. I felt some reprieve from the chaos of my life when I stayed with my mother. She was eighteen years into her recovery from alcoholism, and although it was torture for her when I was there, it helped me.

On one of those trips I returned to Charlotte to attend a Bruce Springsteen concert with someone I had met at a bar only two weeks earlier on New Year's Eve. The concert was on a Sunday night. I had to teach school on the following day in Charleston. I swore to myself that this night I wouldn't drink. That this night I would enjoy the concert and then make the three-hour drive to Charleston early the next morning. But the expectations of my date, the atmosphere of the concert, and my constant feeling of anxiety and depression were quickly numbed by a first drink. And for most alcoholics, the first drink is the one to fear.

I don't remember the concert or where I stayed that night. I came out of my blackout somewhere along the shoulder of the interstate on the road back to Charleston. I knew I would never make it back to Charleston in time to teach—or be in any kind of state to handle the energy of the classroom. So I called the school from a truck-stop pay phone. "I can't make it today." And the words that followed were the most shameful words I've ever uttered in my life. I told a lie that to this day represents for me the amazing power of alcohol. "Something terrible has happened." The shame possessed me at this point and the lie pushed out as I spoke. "My sister's two children were killed by a drunk driver. I won't be able to make it in until Thursday." "Is there anything we can do?" the concerned voice on the other end of the phone asked desperately. And the robot in me replied, "No."

I hung up, returned to Charlotte, and partied for the next three days.

A fish doesn't know it's in water until it isn't in it anymore. I was never aware of being in the Girl Box—on a conscious level, anyway. But it shaped everything I did.

❏ I always had a boyfriend. This was a requirement of the Girl Box. I wasn't necessarily faithful to my boyfriend, but I always had one. In many instances, though my boyfriend was great, I would sabotage the relationship in search of someone "better." Obviously if he wasn't completing my life, then something was wrong with him. The reason for my discomfort surely couldn't be originating within me. So I would move on to the next man, hoping to be completed by him. Sometimes the person I dated was someone of questionable character. He would lie to me or even hit me. The irony of these relationships was my reluctance to let them go. I would stay in these emotionally (and sometimes physically) abusive relationships because I was going to prove to this person that I was good and could earn his love—or, better yet, make him happy and hence prove my own worthiness.

Relationships required drama. They were either fairy-tale wonderful or movie-star melodrama. In an effort to maintain both, I've: jumped out of a car traveling at thirty-five miles per hour; racked up a $10,000 credit card bill; moved to a new city; grabbed the microphone from band members at a country club dance and yelled obscenities; threatened suicide; considered plastic surgery; faked illness; asked someone to marry me; threatened leaving.

❏ I always had to look good. In eighth grade I still didn't have my period. I hadn't yet hit a hundred pounds and was incredibly self-conscious of my unfeminine appearance. I can remember holding the library door open for a guest at my school who said, "Thank you, sir." I was mortified. I went to the bathroom and slammed my fist into the wall.

The summer before my junior year in college I worked at a summer camp on the coast of North Carolina. I started running in earnest then, and I was beginning to look like a real athlete. My hair took on a lighter shade of summer and my skin a golden coat of sunshine. I returned to college and within one week was getting attention like I had never known.

I didn't realize it, but the message was in there: Look good and the boys will like you. I had known this all along, but I had never experienced it firsthand. But now—wow!—people were talking about how I had changed over the summer, and wasn't I looking good, and what was I doing to have blossomed like that. I was no different than the year before—other than my looks—and suddenly the attention was overwhelming. I wasn't prepared for it. At last I had it and I didn't like it. "I'm still in here," the real person inside would say, but the boys didn't want to hear her. They wanted the summer blond and the toned body. At least that's what the Girl Box told me they wanted. So that's what I gave them.

Thus, the next several years were spent making an effort to always maintain appearances—not because it made me feel good, but because I received the attention I had always longed for. I was a full-blown inhabitant of the Girl Box now. I spent countless hours molding my body into what society considered beautiful. I'd lift weights, drink protein shakes, restrict my diet—all in an attempt to create the perfect body. I've always been thin and incredibly self-conscious of it. Ironically I was always attempting to create more body, more muscle. I would wish for more breast, more roundness. And other than plastic surgery, the only way to do this for a thin person was with exercise, weight lifting, and diet.

This past holiday season on a rare Southern snowy day, I was running on the treadmill at my local YMCA. A woman running on the treadmill next to me was talking to a friend who was standing in front of the treadmill. For thirty minutes they talked about how "bad" they had been over the holidays. "I've really got to get back into this whole exercise thing again," she said. "I've done nothing but eat bonbons and cheesecake over the holidays. I am so fat." For thirty minutes they discussed what they had eaten, how bad they had been, and how they intended to work it off in the next few days. I ached for this woman, having been where she is. I wondered to myself if she had seen her children's eyes sparkle when Santa Claus had left his gifts or if she and her husband had shared some moments of intimate gratitude as they rang in the New Year. But all I knew about this woman was that she had eaten "bad" foods, was condemning herself for it, and was going to punish it off of her body. She was letting life simply float right by her.

❑ In the Girl Box I had to keep quiet. I am a smart person. I won the Senior of the Year award at my high school, went on to an excellent university, and graduated with a degree in chemistry. I was a member of a well-known academic fraternity. But I never took satisfaction in it. Smart girls were too boylike. Girls were supposed to be pretty—sexy—not smart, and if you *were* smart you'd best keep those smarts inside. So I gave up the smart side of myself and spoke the script of the flirtatious, silly girl. I relinquished the depth of intelligence and got very good at small talk and shallow conversation.

When I was twenty-four, I attended a function with a professor at a military college. It was at the president of the college's home and most attendees were at least twenty years my senior, including my date. I get tickled when I revisit the picture he and I painted when we walked into the semiformal event. He had on a tuxedo. I had on a leopard-print pair of pants and a midriff that revealed my belly button and a good bit of the territory around it. I remember walking into the president's backyard and the entire (yes, I said entire) throng of people turning to look at us. Kevin smiled one of those sly cat-smiles, and I remember feeling a strange mixture of "This is what I want, but this is not what I want." I didn't know any other way. Women are to be admired. I got what I wanted. Kevin got what he wanted. But I realized at that instant that no one would talk to me—really talk to me. The moment presented a strange mixture of power and sorrow. Look at me, but don't look at me. Admire me, but don't admire me. Please think I'm pretty, but don't think I'm pretty.

I think I said twenty words the whole night. I was picture-perfect and afraid to open my mouth, trapped in the Girl Box again.

So, just like when I was five years old, the incompleteness, the feeling of not being good enough, followed me everywhere—and I was a full participant in creating the box that would affirm the feelings of inadequacy and incompetence I had all the time.

On July 6, 1993, I hit bottom. I was homeless, jobless, relationship-less, ill, lonely, and deafened by that shameful cancer growing inside of me. I wanted to die. The lid to the Girl Box was seven feet above me and I placed a last-ditch call to my sister. "Lift me out, please, somebody, anybody!" that little girl in there was calling. She had heard this from me many times and, as always, she was patient: "Molly, just sleep on it.

Promise me that you will just sleep on it—see how you feel in the morning."

So I set aside the knife I had pulled from the kitchen drawer and curled up in the fetal position on the couch. I lay there in the despair, in the silence and the darkness of the Girl Box, and knew that nothing short of a miracle would pull me out of that wished-for sleep.

The following evening, somehow, I dragged myself out the door and by rote hit the pavement for my daily run. The air was electric with a coming thunderstorm, the wind blowing the leaves of the trees upside down and causing the dirt on the street to swirl up. Rounding the last corner of my six-mile run onto East Boulevard, I was on the last stretch of road toward the apartment where I was staying. Everything was in sync, my breathing, the float of my steps on the pavement, my relaxed arms, my speed—and as I approached the intersection of Kenilworth and East Boulevard I moved from total effortless to breathlessness, overcome with the moment. Something was happening—something so real, so raw, so momentous, it forced me to stop dead in my tracks at that intersection. The sounds of the city floated to the background, the street disappeared, and like tunnel vision I became fixated on the way the sun filtered through the leaves on the trees, casting the most distinct shadows on the pavement at my feet. I could hear my breathing, my heartbeat in my ears; feel the sweat flowing across my temples and down my back and chest; a surge of strength, power, *presence* lit me up—and in that instant my life changed. Call it what you want, but the darkness of the shame I had hidden away inside was warmed by a light of such power that for that moment I just *was*: present, pure, and worthwhile.

I ran home, totally confident in the knowing that things would be different. That every step from here on would be intentional and connected to that presence.

I stopped drinking and sought support for my recovery, and my life started to get better right away. I began to take care of the things that were nagging me. I made payment arrangements with people to whom I owed money. I woke up without hangovers and discovered the morning.

A job opportunity came up several months later that put me into the alcohol and substance abuse prevention field and into a very healthy working environment. I returned to the sport of triathlon and discovered a different way to approach competition. Healthy people began to be part of my circle of friends—many of them in recovery themselves.

I began to seek the presence I had felt on that run in everyone I met and in everything I did: songs on the radio, the shape of a cloud, a smile from a child, the girl at the McDonald's drive-through window. The spirit I'd felt during that run was actually everywhere. Everywhere! And all I had to do was open my eyes to see it, take it in. And so the shame in there began to be less important. The world I was discovering in those early months of sobriety was *not* a world that affirmed the shame I carried around—it was not a world that supported the Girl Box. The world I was discovering was a world where people were genuine, grateful, humble, authentic, honest, enthusiastic, warm, giving, and reliable. This new world operated on a completely different wavelength. People in this world seemed to be connected to a completely different power source than the one which I had plugged into all those years. This source transmitted the message that wholeness was achieved not by expecting approval from others but by accepting one's worth—the worth that is simply inherent in each of us the day we are born.

Early sobriety was for me a time of incredible celebration and awakening. I found joy in the smallest things—paying my water bill, waking up without a hangover, making all of the traffic lights on my way to work.

Now don't get me wrong. Sobriety didn't get me out of the Girl Box forever. My abuse of alcohol was simply one way to cope with the stifling box. When I think I have it tackled, another issue pops up that forces me to take stock. As with an onion, I peel one layer away and suddenly I discover an entirely new layer that needs examination.

I will never be able to fully explain what happened on that July run. What I do know is this: For one brief instant the little girl in there that I had denied a voice, a body, and acceptance all those years was discovered. I welcomed her into the present and set her free from the Girl Box.

There have been only a few times since then that I have had that kind of deep connection, totally free of the Girl Box.

Pregnancy would be one of those. I knew the moment I conceived my two children, Hank and Helen. Within seconds of their small souls entering my body, I knew—and while I was pregnant with them I felt that connection; the incredible responsibility of nurturing a spirit in my body; and in doing so for those nine months, celebrated mine. I was full, round, and focused on the process. I read all of the books and charted their progress with each passing day. Pregnancy was like having one foot in heaven and one on earth. I delivered both of my children without the use of drugs, intentionally. I wanted to be as present as possible for the experience. I remember the unbelievable pain, the involuntary groans, the fluids that leaked from my body. My husband held my hand, talked me through each contraction. I could sense that my children were intensely involved in the process, working with me. And then, the miracle of birth. Time stood still and what was at one time only a spirit took human form into this human world. I remember pulling Hank and three years later, Helen, to my breast and their natural ability to suckle. I remember how the rest of time and space stopped and they were all that mattered. For those two instants all that mattered was my looking into their eyes and theirs looking into mine. I was a woman. I was a mother. I was complete.

I remember one particular night, eleven months after Hank was born. It was late August in North Carolina. He had awakened in the middle of the night and I walked in the dark to his crib, lifted him into my arms, and settled into the rocking chair by his window. A thunderstorm was building and I nursed him. The lightning brightened his face and the soothing rumble of distant thunder warmed the room. He fell asleep in my arms and I sat there for another good hour, just rocking him, listening to the thunder and feeling peaceful and present.

I still try to capture those moments with my children. I often feel that connection with them in the morning. Helen will slowly descend the stairs and peek around the corner of the living room. I hear her tiny steps coming and leave the work at my computer and rush to the couch as if I've been waiting there all morning for her. She runs to my arms and I hold her like a baby again. Even Hank lets me hold his sturdy seven-year-old boy-body in my arms as if he were an infant again, his head cradled in my left arm and his legs draped across my right. The morning sun sieves through the blinds and gently rests across his growing body. We look at each other, Hank and I—or Helen and I—and for that instant all is right with the world.

I'm a single mother now, and those moments of clarity and peace are harder to find as I rush about trying to hold it together. One recent summer night, the children were asleep in bed. I had washed up the dinner dishes, been grocery shopping that day, paid my bills and still had a little money in my checking account. I can remember going out on the front porch with a cup of sweet iced tea. A neighbor had just cut his grass and the greenness of it filled my senses. Lightning bugs were dancing in the dusk air and the crickets were beginning to sing. I sat there in the stillness and felt the calm fall down over me, draped across my shoulders by the moment.

I always get a sense of that kind of peace when I deliver the Girls on the Run program. I admire the honesty of those little girls and cherish their unconditional love. I can't remember my own fourth grade, but I can find the lost memories by creating new ones through Girls on the Run. I can feel that sense of peace that comes in knowing that little girls have a perfect spirit; that my spirit was perfect then and is perfect now. I give the little girl in me the love she yearned for when she was younger. I am present for her. I love her. I feel reunited with her and whole.

Working to stay out of the box is just that: work. I have had to work very hard to recognize the messages there and to be aware when I am giving in to them. Being aware of them doesn't make the thoughts just go away, though. I have to *do* something.

Here are some of the personal steps I take to climb out of the Girl Box.

CONNECT WITH THE PRESENCE

First and foremost, I make time every morning to connect with that presence. Sometimes it is only for five minutes; other times it is an entire weekend. But I consciously ask for guidance throughout the day from the power of It and trust that I will, once I connect, do the next right thing.

I picture my life like an in-box, full of to-dos, exciting opportunities, and challenges. The night I hit bottom, my in-box had one item to do: "feel your powerlessness." So the day after my epiphany I took five minutes to try to connect with my Higher Power. Ironically, the in-box began to get more requests. And as the requests for personal progress began to increase in my in-box, so did the need for more time to consciously seek contact with my Higher Power. The professional opportunities and challenges have also multiplied in my in-box. Now I am seeking guidance with nearly each breath in and out. For years I kept thinking that if only I could get that in-box empty, I would be content. If only I was pretty enough, rich enough, smart enough, true happiness would follow. But my Higher Power doesn't work like that. The in-box will never be empty; hence I am forced to grow with each new request, each new challenge, each new opportunity—and I cannot progress without seeking the guidance of It. The requests in the in-box have changed over the years. In early sobriety, they were "pay back the money you owe," "get a good job," "take care of your health." Now the requests are more internal in nature. "Be true to yourself." "First things first." "One day at a time." "Celebrate yourself." "Know you are loved."

WRITE A GRATITUDE LIST

I close each day with a gratitude list. My life is so full of what I have, and the more I focus on it, the more "haves" I get. My family, my children, my health, Girls on the Run, my house, my car, my smile, my emotions—that list is infinite in length and in its power to lift me up.

REMIND MYSELF OF MY ABILITY TO CONTROL MY PERCEPTIONS

So much of that shame back then (and I still struggle with it, don't get me wrong) was based on other people's perceptions of me. Surely I wasn't responsible for my mother's drinking, but a third grader doesn't understand that and she was, after all, *my* mother. Likewise, as I grew into womanhood, all of those Girl Box issues were external in nature—be pretty, be thin, have money, have the right man, be the best mother, take care of everyone else's needs—all of that "stuff" is based on what other people think. And what I learned in that moment during that run was that the only person over whom I have control is myself. There is a prayer that pulls me through any difficult time. It is the Serenity Prayer: "God, grant me the serenity to accept the things I cannot change, the courage to change the things I can, and the wisdom to know the difference." Early on in my sobriety I learned this prayer and would repeat it to myself in my darkest moments. Restated, what it means to me is that I have no control over other people, places, and things, but I do have control over how I choose to perceive them. No one else has that control over me.

MAKE AMENDS TO THOSE I MAY HAVE HURT

I've hurt a lot of people over the years. Alcoholics do that. My mother did it to me. We all do it, whether we are alcoholic or not. I did it to most of the people with whom I came in contact. Not necessarily purposefully—the power of the alcohol made me something I wasn't. But in order for me to move on it was absolutely necessary for me to make a list of all of the people I had harmed (including myself) and share this darkness with someone. In my case it was one of my good friends who was also in recovery. When it was appropriate or wouldn't hurt the other person, I would call or write the individuals on that list and apologize to them. If I owed someone money I would work out an arrangement with them if I couldn't pay the total immediately. This process freed me to look people in the eye, unload some of that shame that the alcohol had nourished, and move on with a clean slate.

Now I do this every day. At the end of each day—or, even better, the instant it happens—I do a quick spot-check and, if I have harmed someone, try to amend the situation immediately. Sometimes the fear of rejection or conflict rears its ugly head and I avoid the person whom I've harmed, but inevitably this will feed that shame and I have to eventually make amends to the person. Retiring at night with my life slate clear and straight allows me to sleep peacefully and wake up to the sunshine of the next day. "The beginning is always today." (Mary Wollstonecraft)

KEEP A JOURNAL

Through journaling I began to recognize some themes to my life. Seeing these patterns didn't help me explain *why* I did things a certain way, but they did show me *how* I did certain things and, hence, allowed me to address healthier ways of managing my life. People pleasing has always been a huge issue for me and has been a major theme throughout my life. People pleasing is one of the biggest falsehoods of the Girl Box. In the Girl Box, we live in a constant circus of trying to get other people to like us. We aren't okay the way we are, so we keep seeking that okayness from others. I selfishly thought in some way that I could influence someone else's perception of me by behaving in a particular way. The problem with this perception is the motive. Am I behaving honorably so that you will love me or because I will feel love? When I was in the box, my motive for most everything I did was to be loved—now my motive is higher-powered and is more focused on feeling love. Love is ever-present and it is my job to act in a manner that allows me to feel it, regardless of others' actions or perceptions of me.

EXPERIENCE AND SHARE MY WORTH

I began to feel my own worth. It didn't happen right away, but my improved self-esteem began to flow all through my work, my athletic life, my personal life. And as my sense of worth began to grow stronger in me, I felt that I had to share it with others. This is why and how Girls on the Run was born. Girls on the Run has given me a far greater reason for living—and I believe the seed of it was planted in my very being with the pain of my mother's drinking, my own drinking, and, subsequently, the freedom I experienced on that run and all of the other events of my life. I daily try to share the power of my own presence with others so that it gives them permission to feel their own and share it with others. Instead of staying in the shame and the self-deprecating life of the victim, I have chosen to live a life of strength, hope, and optimism.

It was out of this feeling of worthiness that Girls on the Run grew. I knew that I wasn't alone in that box. There are thousands and thousands of girls and women suffocating in there. So in 1996 I took the greatest risk of my life. I wrote a simple version of the current curriculum and tried it out with thirteen very brave little girls at a school in Charlotte, North Carolina.

The click was immediate. They were energized and so was I. We longed to be with one another, sharing, laughing, running, skipping, and learning. Here was the safety I had longed for, the place where I could be in fourth grade all over again as I had dreamed it would be for myself. I could create the fourth grade

I'd lost in my mother's alcoholism, my low self-esteem, and my shame, and relive it the way all fourth graders should experience it. In only two hours per week I was able to reclaim the little girl that had gotten lost in there and celebrate her with her friends.

In the first year, the program grew to seventy-six participants throughout Charlotte with an ever-growing waiting list. Something great was at work here. Soon we began to get some press and Girls on the Run went national. Colorado, Tennessee, Virginia . . . by word of mouth the program began to spread, and today the numbers continue to grow exponentially. There are numerous full-time staff members handling the daily operations—all of whom grasp the Girls on the Run concept at the very core of their own souls. Girls on the Run folks not only talk the talk, they walk the walk.

DANCE!

Lastly, one of the most important activities I do to keep myself out of the Girl Box is to spontaneously dance a lot. Around my house, alone and with my children, during Girls on the Run, in the car, in my office, when I run, I dance a lot and whenever I feel like it. Just watch a fourth-grade girl. She can't go for very long periods of time without moving her body in some graceful but silly way. Dancing for me is the complete uninhibited celebration of body, spirit, personality, senses, energy, silliness, eccentricity, authenticity, realness, life—everything that I wasn't prior to that July 7 run. "We should consider every day lost in which we do not dance at least once." (Friedrich Nietzsche)

The steps for freeing myself from the Girl Box and living an authentic and real life are simple and few in number, but I constantly take them. Just when I think one area of my life is moving along comfortably and peacefully, something happens that forces me to take a deeper look into myself—another more challenging item hits my in-box.

I've finally figured out that for me, the process of life boils down to one simple lesson: "Letting go and letting it show." Housed in this physical body is my spirit. Growing older is simply the process of letting go of passing relationships, children, careers, physical beauty, youth, and my physical body to unveil and let show the beauty that lies within.

What makes me beautiful is my story, the shame that molded the strong woman I am today, the sunshine that claimed that place inside of me, the Presence with which I have daily contact, and the little-girl spirit in there that dances, uninhibited, joyfully, simply, and present in the moment.

My daughter Helen, only four, is still very much surprised by her body and the amazing things it can do. She still loves to dance naked around the house—totally uninhibited, surprised when she successfully pulls off a twirling jump on the living-room carpet. "Mommy, look. Mommy, look what I can do!" Her little spirit shines in that beautiful child-body. She dances on my living-room floor with a sparkle in her eye and her tiny toes gripping the floor when she lands. Her arms gracefully follow her body.

Helen's spirit, body, and laugh are one. When she laughs her whole body laughs. When she hugs me, her whole body wraps around mine. When I read her a book, her whole body, her mind, and her energy are completely and totally focused on that book. Taut, engaged, embraced by the words I'm reading to her. She is perfectly content with herself and the minute she is in. Helen is so good at "is-ing."

Helen's skin warm against mine. Her spirit exposed for the world to see. She is teaching me so much. As did my mother, my sister, my friend Jamie who challenged me to fly over that holly bush, and all of the other amazing experiences and people that have intersected my life.

One day just this past week, Helen didn't make her regularly scheduled entrance into the living room. She lay in bed quietly and then in her precious voice called me upstairs. "Mommy, will you come up here?" I went up to her bed.

"Will you snuggle me?" The air in our house was crisp and I pulled myself under the covers. She curled up in the pocket formed by my chest and legs.

"Mommy, I need to tell you something. When I was in heaven, I looked down and saw all the mommies. They were all standing there and I picked you out of all of them. I chose you to be my mommy."

I lay there in the early morning light and tried to absorb what she had said to me. She wrapped her arms around my neck and squeezed tight.

My daughter chose me out of all the other mommies. What an incredible honor. What a gift.

Helen believes that I am good enough, smart enough, beautiful enough, and strong enough.

I am joyously and gratefully beginning to believe it, too.

TWO

A LIFE IN TRAINING

I still can't believe it. Ten years ago, I was empty, purposeless, alcoholic, homeless, and jobless. I was physically, emotionally, and spiritually bankrupt. Surely I wasn't cut out for a life of such despair. One run, one day, a building thunderstorm, and my life's path was dramatically shifted. The calling was strong and pulled me right into its powerful tentacles.

The story of the program's genesis isn't particularly spectacular, glamorous, or remarkable. The phenomenal growth can be easily broken down into small moments, like snapshots along a time line. Yet, when I consider each of those moments together, they fit perfectly, like the pieces of a puzzle or the patches on a quilt. Each moment wiggles its way into the story and has magically taken me and the program to the next step.

The cobblestones mysteriously led me from one small moment to the next.

When the concept first came to me, I was only one year into sobriety and working at a substance abuse prevention agency in Charlotte. Helen Harrill, my colleague, mentor, and the healthiest person I knew at that time (and still one of the healthiest people I know), welcomed me into the world of responsible but nurturing living. Helen was the first person (other than my mother) who could peer down into my soul and my pain. She would pull the words I needed to say out of me. We would sit for hours, talking, laughing, and sharing. My relationship with her was the first healthy friendship I had ever encountered. (I now have many.) We were, and still are, two people who can share all of themselves—the good, the bad, and the ugly. Her support for my emotional and spiritual growth was a precursor for the necessary risks I had to take to let go of the comfort of that job to create the Girls on the Run program.

The Girls on the Run concept was slow to grow. The shape took two years to form—yet during those two years from 1993 to 1995, I spoke nothing of it. The first time I uttered any acknowledgment of it, I was seated in a Bruegger's Bagels store, munching on a bagel and a bag of chips and drinking a Coke. A woman whom I barely knew at that time but who worked at the school where I used to teach, asked me how I was doing and what I was doing. I shared with her—this almost-stranger—for the first time, my desire to develop a program that fused my love of running with the celebration of little girls' spirits and energy. That was the fall of 1995.

I had, in that seemingly unimportant encounter with my now–close friend Nancy Eringhaus, cast that image out of my mind's eye and into the material world. Slowly the concept began to build momentum—like a star forming, I could feel a larger and larger percentage of my energy shifting from my current job and my own desire to compete in triathlons toward the idea—swirling, enveloping, amassing itself into a targeted, specific program.

So when I actually sat down to write out the lessons while my baby boy slept, they had already been created in some format—in my mind. Writing them was actually a very simple process and took very little time, when I consider the power of those lessons now.

The lessons were clearly coming *through* me—not *from* me.

In the summer of 1996, I drove six hours to the North Carolina coast with my mother, my stepdaughter, and her friend. I was trying to create the name for this "thing," this running program, this character-development concept. "Girls on the Go," "Girls on the Move," "Runnergirl," "You Go Girl" were all possibilities. The words "Girls on the Run" didn't click right away. I remember the exact location on that drive where those words first exited my mouth. "Girls on the Run." Hmmmm. I repeated them over and over and eventually they flowed, they became real, they became.

So I went back to Charlotte Country Day School, the school that I attended and where I had taught, and met with the after-school coordinator, Frank Justice. He had been my adviser when I was a student there. I told him about the program. His comment—and I will never forget it—was, "That sounds cool. Let's throw it out there and see if you can get three or four kids to sign up. You never know."

I created the flyers—hot pink with the annoying words, IT'S FUN, IT'S FIT, IT'S FANTASTIC, AND IT'S JUST FOR GIRLS . . . IT'S GIRLS ON THE RUN! I mailed each of those flyers with a letter explaining the core values of the program to the families of all of the third- and fourth-graders who attended the school. Thirteen mothers called me for more details . . . and thirteen little girls enrolled.

I was ecstatic.

When I started the program, I knew, from the first contact I had with the thirteen little girls who enrolled, that I was on to something amazing. I can vividly remember discussing with a friend during a backpacking trip to the mountains how the program had at last filled me with my reason for being. I shared with him at that time my fantasy about the program becoming nationwide. "Wouldn't it be cool if I could actually make a living at this? Just imagine if other women and men around the country wanted to do this. I could go train them in the concepts and we could affect hundreds of thousands of girls instead of the thirteen I now coach." While I believed in my heart that this was a possibility, I am still completely amazed that my then-fantasy is now a reality.

The following spring, my husband and I moved to a suburb of Charlotte. I determined at that time that I could no longer continue delivering the program. I had only one season under my belt, but the challenges of raising my little boy, the hour-long commute, and a struggling marriage were adding layers of stress upon my already heavy shoulders.

Three mothers of the original thirteen girls called me. They literally begged me to continue the program. They offered more financial support, baby-sitting—anything to get me to continue offering the program. I was going to stick with my *no* response. I picked up the phone to call Sarah Belk—and before I knew what I had done, I let her know that I would definitely continue offering the program and that she and her daughter could look forward to it again in the fall.

The move to this Charlotte suburb had made working at the drug prevention center impossible. Girls on the Run was taking more of my energy and time, so I opted for hourly wage jobs at our local Y and a catering company—the flexible hours allowed me to pursue the program and bring in a little bit of income to our home. I would work at our local Y at 5:30 A.M., offer Girls on the Run after school, and cater at night and into the early hours of the morning. The schedule was hectic, emotionally and physically draining, and terrible for my health. I stayed sick most of that season—two visits to the hospital with pneumonia. I was totally unbalanced and unprepared for the demands of a "calling."

And yet, I had no choice. Callings are like that. I simply had to continue offering the program. The pull of it was strong, powerful, and divinely inspired.

One of the most amazing aspects of Girls on the Run is its rapid rate of growth—from one city to more than a hundred (at the time of this printing) in only six years. All of this so quickly and without any marketing efforts on the part of me or the staff the program now employs. The program just grows. The hundreds of women who now deliver Girls on the Run in their hometowns and cities have their own story of how they learned about the program and how it called to them as it called to me. There is an intuitive "connect" with the precepts of the program.

People either get it or they don't.

Three very key people did get it.

First was Dori Luke. I met Dori at an after-school enrichment program fair—where providers of after-school programming could come tout their wares and coordinators of after-school programs could come learn all about them. Dori was representing an indoor-climbing center. I was representing Girls on the Run.

Neither of us had any takers at our tables. So she walked over to see what Girls on the Run was all about. The click was the most immediate energy exchange I have ever felt with anyone. She got it! I knew a gift had just been handed to me. We exchanged phone numbers.

Dori called me the next week. We met. She had all of the qualifications necessary to assist me in delivering the program.

She had experience in facilitating groups, she understood experiential learning, she was an athlete. She was the most important "next step" in reaching more girls than those I could directly influence.

Not too long after I met Dori, I had a bout with strep throat. I called Dori and asked her to substitute for me at one of my sites. She did.

Upon my return the girls were asking, "When can Dori come back?" "Dori played some really fun games with us." "Can she come help you more often?" I asked Dori if she would like to sign on next season as a Girls on the Run coach. We could expand the program to three more locations and reach sixty more little girls. She jumped at the chance. The following fall, Girls on the Run expanded to five sites and enrolled seventy-six girls.

I don't believe in coincidence. Meeting Dori was not a coincidence.

Dori was definitely a gift. What I didn't know at the time of our meeting was the fact that her mother, Sue Luke, was a nationally known specialist in the field of eating disorders. Sue Luke served on numerous national boards and had worked with adolescent girls for her entire adult life. She traveled extensively throughout the country speaking on the struggles of adolescent girls, contributed to national publications, and was unquestionably an expert in her field.

It was the fall of 1997. Dori asked me if it would be all right if she shared the curriculum with her mother. I said of course, but I was very nervous about an expert in the field examining the curriculum. Would she find out that I'm really an impostor? Would she discover that I don't really know what I'm talking about?

Sue Luke took a look at the curriculum. She called me and asked if she could meet me for coffee at our local Y. I said yes. I

was convinced she would have many suggestions, critically an-
alyze the curriculum, and suggest that I go back to the drawing
board.

I was shaking as I walked into the Y for our meeting. She
was seated by a window that overlooked the playground. I introduced myself, pulled up a chair, and sat directly across from her.

She said, "Let me get right to it." I was prepared for the
worst—sure of a letdown. Ready for the sting.

And then Sue uttered what to me today remain the most
powerful words *anyone* has ever said to me about the Girls on
the Run program. I can feel the chills run across my skin even
now as I write her words. "Molly, what you have here is without question one of the most extraordinary pieces of work I
have ever laid my eyes on. I am awed by it and by you. It seems
to me your biggest question should be not, Is the program
worthwhile? Unquestionably it is one of the most powerful
programs I've ever come across. No, it seems to me your question is, Do I keep it to myself and reach a hundred kids here in
Charlotte . . . or do I give it away and reach millions?"

I cried. Right there, on the spot—in that moment. The last
bit of fear that I had carried with me regarding the future of the
program simply vanished. I felt the presence of God—knew
that the spirit of this program was powerful and real. I knew,
without a doubt, that I had to let it go.

Strangely, the joy was tempered by a sense of burden: the
responsibility of it; the demands this growing program would
put on me and my family; the next steps required would ex-
haust me, challenge me. I felt as if I was on the edge of something both powerful and painful.

Now enter stage left another woman who got it. In 1998
the senior editor at *Runner's World*, Eileen Portz-Shovlin, called
me in January to let me know that I had received the Golden
Shoe Award. The Golden Shoe Award is presented by the inter-

nationally distributed publication to someone who has contributed to his or her community through running. When the call came into my house, I was exhausted. I was barely pregnant with Helen. Hank was napping. I covered the mouthpiece of the phone with my hand and listened to her while holding back a joyous yelp. This was just too much. I felt my heart bursting with joy.

In June of 1998 the small article appeared in *Runner's World*. I was four months pregnant in the photograph, with luscious apple-red cheeks, and so unknowing then of the changes my life was about to undergo with that brief but far-reaching description of me and the program.

A few days after the magazine hit newsstands a remarkable woman, Lisa Ledet, called me from Colorado. "I saw the feature on your program in *Runner's World*. Have you ever thought about expanding the program?" "Of course I have," I replied. So Lisa, along with two others—Lee Hartline from Virginia and Jody Worth from Tennessee—traveled to Charlotte to learn about the program.

Only a few months earlier, Dori had begun to help me translate the curriculum from "Molly language" into a format that anyone could understand. Her work toward creating the curriculum we know today was one of the most important contributions to the Girls on the Run program. Only days before the out-of-state women came to Charlotte, she and I sat in her mother's house and printed out the first edition of the Girls on the Run curriculum. What had been in Molly language was now in a language that could be understood by all. We could touch it.

And so in August of 1998, only six weeks before my daughter Helen was born, the program was introduced to the rest of the world. Like my daughter, the Girls on the Run program left the safe womb of my direct control and was placed into the hands of the divine. The program was now a living, breathing, *real* agent of change. On its own, sustained by the care of others. I remember weeping painfully from a deep place of overwhelming fear the night after those three women left.

I felt as if a piece of me had been ripped from my very being. And so, like that brilliant July run, I paused in that emotional whirlwind to sit in its epicenter and meditate on the wonder of it—seek the divine and acknowledge the fact that following a calling is never easy. The only way the program could grow, nurture, and provide love to millions of girls was for me to simply let it go.

Lisa and the two other women who took Girls on the Run back to their communities called me a lot. They had my home phone number and used it. We had a very skeletal contract. I am forever grateful for their honesty in their delivery of the program. Basically, they left with a handshake and their promise to deliver it in a manner in keeping with the values of the program.

The number of path-altering moments has been so many and so frequent, it would be impossible to list them all here. Now we have four full-time employees in our national headquarters and are hiring a fifth. Elaine Miller, our national director, was an attorney who had the courage to quit her financially stable job at a law firm to coach Girls on the Run—to let go of her Girl Box expectations so that she could spend more time with her daughter and take "Elaine time." She needed to discover who she was as a woman. Slowly but surely the number of Girls on the Run responsibilities on her list began to increase. In 2001 she became the national director.

Sidney Povall, our operations director, was also called to the program. A former inhabitant of the Girl Box, Sidney decided courageously to tackle some of her fears and served as a Girls on the Run coach for a couple of years. Like Elaine, her responsibilities began to increase over that time frame and when the job of director of operations needed to be filled, her life provided her with good timing, emotional health, and a willingness to follow *her* calling.

Most encounters with the people who work with our organization have been like that. Lisa Perry, an employee at New Balance, was reading a magazine one evening and came across a small story about the program. The program clicked for her. She called us and we now have corporate sponsorship from New Balance athletic shoes.

Our Webmaster's sister directs our Charlotte program. Our largest contributor has grandchildren in the program—I coached her daughter—and she gave me my first book on William Glasser.

Our board chair is a woman against whom I used to compete and who has two daughters who have completed the program.

One nationally syndicated radio personality enrolled his daughter and now does free spots for the program.

I was on an NPR syndicated talk show and the host introduced me to the woman who is now my literary agent, Jenny, who connected with our concept right away. She helped me reach the publishing houses in New York City and the editor who has edited this book feels pulled to the precepts of the program. She gets it!

The coincidences, the exchanges, the connections continue to link each of us to one another. Heck, *you* are reading this book—you are now a part of this connection, this band of rebels who seeks to make it okay to shop at Target, considers cellulite a normal and beautiful part of a woman's body, *and* uses beauty as a verb.

I'm betting you have a story of how you heard about this

book—the moment something in the telling about it clicked for you, that aha moment when you said, "I just have to read it." This is how underground movements get started.

The path continues to widen. We are actively negotiating with and recruiting new sponsors. What once was as simple as a handshake and a phone call is now a fairly complicated contractual agreement, a two-day training, and periodic site visits. Girls on the Run 5K events now exist in cities across the country, and thousands and thousands of little girls are directly involved with the program. We've been in *Runner's World* two additional times, as well as *People*, *ESPN*, and countless other magazines and newspapers across the country.

I still coach a group of fifteen girls in my hometown. I still remember the names of every girl I have coached. I still have such a long way to go to get out of the Girl Box. I'm still amazed at what powerful teachers little girls can be. I still walk away from each day at my office refreshed, grateful, and completely dumbfounded at the path my life now takes.

To have known such despair—to have stared at my pained reflection in the silver blade of a knife ten years ago—and to now see my reflection in the eyes of my children . . . such joy is unimaginable.

I was paralyzed by my fear back then. And now—well, now I am not fearful anymore. I've learned that if I just take a step forward, the cobblestone will appear.

THREE

SHE'S IN THERE

Since the birth of Girls on the Run, I've had the privilege to work with hundreds of girls—girls who are still comfortable in their own bodies, who are amazed at the beauty of their own skin and the sun-kissed freckles that spill across their nose in summer, who thrill at the first trickle of dewy sweat as it rises from their pores, who delight in stomping in brown puddles and running in the rain, who marvel at the way thick, squishy mud oozes up through running shoes onto white socks and into the pockets formed by the delicate curves of their little girl feet.

I know girls. I know their hope.

AMANDA'S QUESTION

Now that Girls on the Run has transformed into an international nonprofit, I am often in the company of attorneys. Karl, my attorney, is a nationally known trademark attorney, and his wife, Pam, is a dynamic, outgoing woman. They were at dinner one evening with their four-year-old daughter, Amanda, when the discussion of careers came up. Karl and Pam were telling their daughter, "Honey. You can be anything you want to be when you grow up—a mommy, a lawyer like your daddy, an astronaut, a banker, even the president of the United States. What do you think you want to be?" Amanda pondered the question. After a few seconds of considering their query, she asked, "Do they still have queens?"

And you know what I would tell her? A resounding, "Yes they do!" Maybe not in the traditional sense, but every woman, every girl has within her a queen just poised to emerge.

The key is finding her in there.

Finding the queen inside us is a difficult task nowadays. We get slammed with a variety of messages that tell us just how that queen should act and what she should look like.

But I'm hopeful. She is in there and she is wonderful!

I have read countless journals, research studies, and pop-culture books on girls. They all provide me with an array of resources for helping girls rediscover the queen that resides inside their souls. Heck—they help ME rediscover the queen that resides inside MY soul.

And yet, the power of what I learn directly from the girls themselves—the stories that follow—provides a wealth of knowledge that can only come from the source of peace I felt on that July run. Children have the uncanny knack for saying just what they feel and, in doing so, speak a truth that comes from their hearts—the center of their souls. The research is very important (see the following chapter); yet it is the inspiration, the hope, the girlspeak that resonates with me—that teaches me what I need to do to encourage each little queen to peek from inside the Girl Box and step into the sunshine.

What do I need to do to free the queen inside of me? Let her step out in all her glory.

TINA'S STORY

Tina is in fifth grade. Tina is a big girl—some of the other girls in her class call her fat. Tina is about five two and probably weighs about 160 pounds. Tina has attitude—she sometimes puts other kids down as a defense for the name calling, the hurtful words, and the stigma of being the fat girl. When Tina reads magazines, all the models are thin, beautiful, and sexy. They all have nice cars and don't have to work when they are fifteen. All those actresses she reads about wear makeup, smoke cigarettes, and confuse her because her mama—a good, strong woman—tells her that "That stuff ain't good for you," but she thinks maybe if she tries it she'll be beautiful, too.

Tina is in Girls on the Run.

Two thirds of the way through the twelve-week program, the girls get a chance to practice a 5K (3.1-mile) run or walk. They have the entire hour session to complete the three miles. Tina did not believe she could do it. So, like most frightened queens, she decided not to try. When her coach yelled, "Go," Tina began strolling very slowly around the track. While the majority of girls in the group were running by her, I could see the queen in Tina look on with envy: "My body can never do this."

Thirty minutes into the one-hour session, Tina had strolled one and a quarter miles. Her coach walked the next lap with her and gently pointed out that at this rate she wouldn't finish. But if she could just increase her steps a few more per minute, she would. Tina still had attitude but, whether she liked it or not, she was walking a little bit faster as her coach paced her through the next mile.

Now Tina had done two miles. She had about fifteen minutes to go.

All the other girls had already finished.

Among them was Jordan. Jordan is the fastest runner. She is skinny and in third grade. Jordan always finishes first. Jordan noticed something special on that day. She noticed that Tina had gone farther than she ever had. She walked to the edge of the track. "Tina, you've gone farther than you ever have. Come on, you can do it," she yelled joyfully.

And in that moment, I witnessed a light—*the* light—sparkle in Tina's eyes. The queen emerged. The realization of "I can do this" transformed her stroll into a jog, her attitude into a kick, and her body into a machine. With every ounce of her being, Tina started jogging, then running, huffing and puffing every step of the way. She smiled with each stride—moving that big, strong, bold body effortlessly around the pavement.

Before the last lap was complete, all sixteen girls had joined her. She had done it. The body that never would, could. A smile full of sunshine stretched across that beautiful brown face as sweat broke out on her brow.

On that day, Tina took her body back. She took it back from the magazines, from the movies, and from the MTV images. She took her body back from the teacher who told her she was lazy and from the fourth grader who called her fat with a tinge of disgust. Tina took her body back. Big. Strong. Beautiful. Bold. Her body is her body and she took it back.

Tina's lesson: Every opportunity I have to celebrate the strength, boldness, and beauty of my body, my children's bodies, the girls' bodies—I take it. I ask my daughter to admire her form in the mirror—every part of her: the strength of her little legs, the roundness of her toddler belly, the dimples at the base of her back, the curl of her toes.

In Girls on the Run, I acknowledge out loud to the girls the miracle of their bodies, the flow of their hair behind them, and the unique ways they carry their bodies through space. I help each girl make the connection between her beautiful spirit and how it shines out through the hop in her step, the swing of her arms, and the sparkle in her eyes.

Every morning, I include a moment or two during my quiet time to thank my body for the amazing things it does every day—the way it gives me time to have a conscious connection with my soul, the gift that it is, and the value in it.

What I learned from Tina: Celebrate my daughter's body.

MADDIE'S STORY

Maddie is in third grade. Her hair always sticks up, shiny blond from too much swimming-pool chlorine and sun. Her little knees are knobby, her small ribs show through the muscle of her small frame. Maddie is tiny. Her voice is tiny. Her socks always fall down around her ankles and her shoes are always untied. She wears glasses that look like Coke bottles and has obvious problems with coordination.

Maddie is in Girls on the Run.

Maddie, born with congenital heart issues as an infant, is a fighter. But there she was, sticking-out hair, falling-down socks, and the spirit of someone special. The only problem was that her heart was starting to not work right again. She was getting weaker, losing weight, and having problems even walking through the games. Tears would well up in her eyes, so frustrated was she with the body that houses her strong spirit.

Three weeks before the culminating 5K run/walk in which all of the girls in her hometown were participating, Maddie's parents rushed her to the hospital after she collapsed at home.

The doctors opened up the body that housed that strong little-girl spirit, held her beating heart in their hands, corrected the weakness there, and ever so gently placed her life back into her body. Maddie's spirit was renewed now—a better-than-ever heart pumping the blood of her very life back into her tiny body.

And three weeks after her heart had been cut open, exposed and vulnerable, Maddie ran in that 5K with six hundred other Girls on the Run. She crossed that finish line in fifty-three minutes, arm in arm with her friends.

She was crying.

She had done it.

Maddie got her spirit back that day. It had never really been taken, just scared of dying, scared of a body that wasn't working right anymore, scared and hiding behind the queen. On that day, Maddie's spirit soared for all of her friends to see. Thousands of spectators at that 5K remarked about what an inspiration it was to see this knobby-kneed third grader. Thousands of men and women watched that little soldier cross the finish line and found their own spirits that day. The kings and queens hiding inside peered out—permission at last to step into the sunshine.

Maddie's lesson: Every opportunity I have to celebrate the spirit that is unique to each of us—I take it. I constantly reinforce, immediately, when a girl does something that shows strength of character. Whether she returned an item she found, helped me by carrying my bag, cheered on her friends, stopped to help someone who had fallen, I let her know that I saw the goodness of her spirit and just how amazing it is.

I acknowledge out loud to my own children when they speak kind words about another person, encourage each other, or thank me for something I've done. I help them make the connection between the beauty of their spirit and how it manifests itself through their actions and thoughts.

I take time every morning to find the goodness in myself, hold it in my hands—as Maddie's doctors did with her beating heart—examine it, and thank my spirit for it. I celebrate the uniqueness of *my* spirit—the gift that it is, and the value in it.

What I learned from Maddie: Celebrate my daughter's spirit.

SUSAN'S STORY

The year was 1997. I was still the only coach delivering the Girls on the Run program. Here I was, juggling a struggling marriage, a two-year-old son, and this expanding nonprofit. Seventy-six girls were enrolled in the program and I was coaching three sets of twenty-five girls at each. I traveled two hours a day in a commute that was growing longer due to the rapid growth in suburban Charlotte, the stress was mounting, and I was wondering how I could possibly continue at this pace.

Girls on the Run was my reprieve from the pressure—the spot in the day where I could become present in the moment—celebrate the goodness in myself and my life and shed, if only for an hour, the darkness I felt more frequently in my personal life.

I won't ever forget Susan. Susan was small, quiet, and a loner. She wasn't chatty like most third-grade girls. She was usually engrossed in a book and was clearly the scapegoat of her class. Every day that we came together in our Girls on the Run Getting on Board circle, Susan would position herself, cross-legged, several feet away from the circle, book in hand, and back to us.

And every day, I'd call her over, pat the ground next to me, and say, "Susan, I've got a seat saved, right here, just for you. See?" And without fail, Susan would look up as if startled that I had called her over, gently close the book, and move to sit next to me.

Novembers in North Carolina are hit or miss. They have a saying here: "If you don't like the weather, wait a minute." This particular November day was spectacular. Fire-red leaves remained in piles around maple trees, and the track where we ran was coated with them, like fresh red paint. The lesson scheduled for that day was on community, but I opted for something different.

Four weeks earlier, I had learned of my pregnancy—a child was growing inside of my healthy body and tumultuous life. This was the day I would tell them—I would welcome this child into the arms of my Girls on the Run family.

For the workout, I took nine Popsicle sticks and wrote each of the following individual words on one stick: *Molly, is, going, to, have, a, baby, in, July.* I mixed up the sticks and told the girls that they were going to receive a stick for each lap they ran. The sticks had some very special words on them. At the conclusion of the lesson, the girls would take all the sticks and put them in sequential order to make a sentence that would let them in on a very special secret! This required them to cooperate with one another.

The anticipation was enough to keep them moving briskly for thirty-five minutes. Anxiously I called them back. Quickly the girls lined up the sticks and someone yelled "Molly is going to have a baby." All twenty-five precious girls ran to me and began caressing my still-flat belly; in sweet high-pitched voices they would cup their mouths with their hands and talk to the growing child inside of me. "Hello, babeeeeeeee!" they squealed. Little ears and small girl hands were gently placed on my skin, beneath my shirt. The warmth of their delight and love for this unborn child brought tears to my eyes. I let them see my vulnerable tears of joy.

My baby died that night. At midnight the telltale cramps of a miscarriage began to pulse through my body and through the night I bade farewell to that small soul.

The next evening I called the families of all of those little Girls on the Run and shared the sad news. I tried to be stoic: "I realize this may be the first encounter your daughter has with death. Maybe you could see this as a teachable moment . . . ," but I was tangled up in my own mourning.

The day I returned to Girls on the Run, those precious children ran to me. Tightly they hugged my neck, held my hand, and stroked my hair. They loved me as they had loved my baby the week before.

We sat in a circle and began to talk. The girls reminisced. "I remember when my grandmother died." One child shared the sad story of her dog's death after being hit by a car. One told of her neighbor's cancer and how she had so far managed to fight it.

An uncomfortable silence developed. The November air was misty, the sky an icy white, and the remaining leaves on the ground were brown and gray. They crackled as the wind blew them down the stretch of track upon which we sat.

And then she spoke. Susan never talked—not much, anyway. "I'm so sorry that your baby died. I'm sure she's in heaven."

I looked at Susan. She looked at me. And for that moment, as brief as it was, I felt a surge of sorrow well up inside my being like none I had ever felt in my entire life. It was as if this little girl was giving me complete permission to let go of this child, this soul that for whatever reason wasn't supposed to be here. Susan gave me permission to acknowledge that in fact—my baby *had* died—and that indeed she was in heaven.

We all sat there very quietly. I cried, the bitter wind chilling the tears on my face. The autumn leaves traced dizzying circles in the white space between us.

I'm quite certain that every girl in that circle felt the impact of that moment.

Susan had found her gift.

Susan had spoken the words that all the others were afraid to say. She had taken that uncomfortable silence and spoken the truth. While her peers were concerned with hurting my feelings or being ridiculed for such an outrageous choice of words, Susan's gift—her courage to speak out what she knew in her heart to be true—empowered all of us seated there. Her bravery gave each of us permission, as we went forward, to find our gifts and celebrate them.

Susan's lesson: Every moment is an opportunity to celebrate another's gifts. It might be acknowledging a person's smile, the way they look me in the eyes when they talk to me, the manner in which they speak positively of others. There is always a gift in what we do.

My daughter's gift is to naturally engage others in her joy, her innocent view of the world, her smile, her uninhibited acknowledgment of her feelings, her presence in just being right where she is, right here, right now.

My son's gift is his unique ability to empathize on a very deep level with others. Hank has this uncanny knack for putting himself into the shoes of another—seeing all sides to a situation. His go-with-the-flow attitude makes him a friend to everyone, and he easily develops rapport both with his friends and my adult friends.

The greatest gift I can give myself is celebrating the gifts I have. I daily acknowledge my strengths in the quiet moments of the morning. In the workplace, I use my gifts to further the organization and relinquish the tasks to which I'm less suited to those who possess a gift for performing them. By celebrating my gifts, I give permission to those around me to do the same with their gifts. Celebrating my gifts with humility is a joyous, uninhibited acknowledgment that I did not *make* my gifts—they were given to me, and my job is to use them to their fullest.

What I learned from Susan: Celebrate my daughter's gifts.

CINDY'S STORY

Each twelve-week Girls on the Run program culminates with the girls participating in a 5K run/walk. Usually groups will piggyback on well-known races within their community. In cities where Girls on the Run is well established, participants run in their very own Girls on the Run 5K event.

Cindy is in Girls on the Run.

She had just completed her first twelve-week session. She has a school of tiny freckles swimming across her nose and stands about four feet high—she's tiny, even for a third grader. She has dirty-blond hair down to her waist that she wears loose.

Cindy's mommy and daddy separated two weeks before the final 5K. Her daddy moved out, for reasons Cindy doesn't understand now—though she may one day, mothers can't explain that kind of pain to a third grader.

Cindy can't put words to the separation yet, though she knows that her life is different—that her mommy is sad and her daddy is gone—and, while the voice of it hasn't come to her yet, the expression in her eyes can't hide the fear, the lack of understanding, the feeling of suspended time, the resettling of it all.

Cindy's mommy and daddy came to watch her run in her big event. They saw their little girl finish her first 5K. They saw determination in her eyes—a blessed substitute for the fear she had carried there lately. I saw Cindy's mommy cry and watched her father try to be stoic. But they were there—for her—to support that little-girl spirit, to watch this child-soul float across the three miles of asphalt.

I took their picture—all three of them. Cindy's daddy asked me to take it.

I wonder what expression the lens caught. Did it see the truth behind their eyes—their love for her little life and the turmoil of their own?

Cindy will remember that day forever. Mommy and Daddy came together for her: They put aside their own drama to watch her do something that allowed her girl-spirit to rise above the pain—for 3.1 miles, anyway—to run with her, to watch her finish.

That memory will be captured in the photo that I had the privilege of taking. My hands molded that picture, framed it in the lens, held the camera steady, and directed. One, two, three, cheese.

Five years ago, Cindy was three. Her mom was pregnant with her little brother. Her parents were in love.

Now they are separated—living separate lives—but they took time to reunite long enough to celebrate the joy of their little girl's accomplishment.

Cindy's lesson: Anything can happen. Anything. But what I know is this: As a parent, I need to try to be ever-present, a ray of light, an instant in time of pure and real joy, for my children who live in the unsettledness, the uncertainty, the confusion the world sometimes places on their shoulders. My job as a parent will remain mine forever—true, real, and welcoming; a place of certainty, warmth, and comfort for my children when the path they walk gets a little rocky.

These past five years have seen a lot of change in my personal life—not all of it easy—but through it the one constant was my mother, my own children, and the little girls who welcomed me, provided me with certainty, warmth, and comfort: the Cindys who unselfishly put aside the chaos of their own world . . .

to step into mine.

What I learned from Cindy: Celebrate the joys of parenthood.

KATHERINE'S STORY

Katherine is only nine years old. She is a typical tomboy—hair unbrushed and usually covered by a baseball cap worn backward. Her high-tops are faded and worn.

Katherine is in Girls on the Run.

A couple of weeks into the program, Katherine told me she could fly. One Friday she showed me how she did it. She marched to the top of a small incline, and—eyes tight, nose scrunched, and arms held out at 90-degree angles—concentrated really hard for a minute. Then, with absolutely no warning at all, she began flapping her arms like a huge pterodactyl and started running— hard—down that small hill. At the bottom, just before it leveled out, she leaped high into the air, and for that moment—breath held, time stopping—Katherine, my nine-year-old friend, took flight. And for that moment I took flight with her.

I remembered that idyllic summer twenty-nine years earlier, before I started sixth grade, when I flew over the Hortons' porch. I remember accepting Jamie's challenge to jump because after all, I was "just a *girl*" and couldn't do all the stuff that boys could do.

I flew over that bush, imagined a swan dive off the cliffs of some exotic island coast, and landed in soft, blue, clear water. Although the landing wasn't nearly so comfortable, beautiful, or glamorous, I flew over that darn bush that day because I believed I could.

Katherine's lesson: Let fly your imagination. Encourage, at every possible moment, your children's imagination. Our imagination is where we create our dreams, our wishes, and our hopes for ourselves.

My children's imaginations are the lands where they try on different lives. One day my daughter, Helen, is a kitty-cat that meows, purrs, and magically talks; the next day she is a mommy to her countless stuffed animals. She beautifully juggles driving them to school, feeding them, bathing them, and putting them to bed—timing their retirement to bed as perfectly as a chef completes the preparation of a multicourse meal. She is successful in her imagination.

Helen also can be an angry teacher in her imagination or a bullying friend. She can try on that "suit" and feel it cover her body and her thoughts. She can learn how to handle the angry teacher or bullying friend by playing one in her imagination.

I remember years ago imagining the Girls on the Run program—and to this date, everything that I envisioned has indeed transpired.

What I learned from Katherine: Celebrate the magic of my daughter's imagination.

LEE'S STORY

Lee is in fourth grade and in Girls on the Run. She arrived the first day at Girls on the Run in her mother's silver Mercedes sedan. In the passenger seat lay numerous fashion magazines—the topmost being *Vogue.* Lee hopped out of the car, skipped to our circle of strength, and sat with her new peers. "I'd like to introduce myself. My name is Molly Barker and I will be your Girls on the Run coach for the next twelve weeks."

A few weeks into the program, Lee followed me to my car. "My mom says I'm fat and ugly. I feel so bad about myself. She wants me to run more so I'll get thin." I looked at this beautiful Asian child and wanted to hold her in my arms and go back to the day she was born and look at the beauty that she was then. An infant, perfect in the eyes of the earth.

"Your mother is wrong. You are not fat. You are beautiful." If only Lee could see herself through my eyes. "My mother is wrong?" She questioned me. "Yes, in my world, you are one of the most beautiful creatures on earth."

Ten years ago, I was eight feet deep into the Girl Box and losing sight of the light above me. The world owed me; it was unfair and a place of lacking. I was ugly, discontent, and miserable. I was inflexible, uptight, and fearful.

The following day, I ran at sunset and was given a new pair of eyes. Eyes that allow me to see both the beauty in Lee and the beauty in her mother as she struggles to fit into a culture that tells her she *isn't* beautiful. I received the gift of positive sight—vision that looks at the glass as not just half full but overflowing. Gratitude fell down upon me—I could run, I had my health, I was complete.

Lee is beautiful. My job is to teach her to see herself as beautiful regardless of what others think—to introduce her to the world I live in and that Girls on the Run is creating for her.

Sometimes we all need reminders.

Lee's lesson: I try to always find the spirit of this positive new world in everything: a song on the radio, a smile from the passenger in the car next to mine at a stoplight, the sunrise, the sunset, a good run, being able to cry when I need to, being able to laugh from my belly, rocking my children to sleep, my mother's death, my successes, and my character defects. I constantly seek the world of the positive. It is all around me and all I have to do is tap into it. It is ever present and always there to lift me up.

Girls on the Run was created to provide girls insight into this world where living is proactive and inspired; where they are celebrated. My job is to positively influence all with whom I come into contact.

Lee's place of lacking reminds me that when I feel like that, I need to dig down deep to the core of why I am here and the many blessings I receive by being here. Being a parent and delivering the Girls on the Run Program lets me live in this world of the positive—to take off my Girl Box blinders and see people for what they really are and the motive behind their actions. I am creating a world where I can celebrate my children, my life, all our little girls, and the little girl inside of me. I am receiving on a daily basis the gifts of this program—the smiles, the hugs, the friendships, the growing, the assessing, the unconditional love of those with whom I come into contact both directly and indirectly. But maybe more important, I receive the gift of positive sight—to accept people where they are and to be accepted. This to me is priceless.

What I learned from Lee: Try to seek the positive in all people and circumstances.

JENNY'S STORY

I had been asked to attend a fund-raiser for a national nonprofit organization. Part of what was offered to the guests was the chance to participate in the Richard Petty Rookie Driving Experience at Lowe's Motor Speedway. (Charlotte is in the heart of

NASCAR racing!) Always willing to try something new, I signed up. I was nervous all day and was actually shaking a little when I arrived at the speedway.

The course was brief. Only two other female athletes were there, along with about twenty NFL former and present football players—all invited guests of this nonprofit organization.

We were split into two groups and driven around the course in a van to experience the twenty-five-percent incline on the curves and get a rundown on the line to take around the track. I felt nervous and excited.

I suited up, put on the crash helmet, and got behind the wheel of that powerful NASCAR vehicle. I pulled down the five-piece seatbelt, familiarized myself with the gearing, and drew the window webbing down next to my face. I was primed on safety features should I need to escape, use the fire extinguisher, or shut the motor off. I then stepped on the accelerator and followed the instructor directly in front of me around the course.

I was alone in that car. The intensity was more than anything I've ever felt before or since. For the minutes I was behind that wheel, every muscle in my body was tense, every ounce of my being was focused on the car in front of me. About two laps into it, I began to shake uncontrollably. The car was strangely quiet with the engine roaring just outside the window and I began to think about Hank and Helen. I wondered how they would feel about their mommy driving so fast. Wouldn't they be scared?

I backed off. I wanted to stop, but had no way to communicate with the instructor leading me through the eight long laps, so I continued and finally pulled into the finish. I climbed out of the window and my legs were shaking. I wanted to leave, to get out of there.

I got into my car to drive home and somewhere before reaching the exit of Lowe's Motor Speedway, I burst into tears. I was crying so hard I actually had to pull the car over to the shoulder.

Jenny was fourteen years old when I met her and living in a small South Carolina town. She'd started smoking when she was eleven and got pregnant when she was thirteen—in fact, I met her when she was pregnant with her little girl. Jenny couldn't drive yet and I was a social worker working her case for the department of social services

I would pick her up, take her to her appointments, and beg her to stop smoking—at least while she was pregnant. She planned to quit school for a while once her cuddly baby was born. Surely her baby would love her. "Babies are so easy," she would say. She and her mama had already bought all of her baby clothes and outfitted a room in their house with a crib and Winnie the Pooh curtains.

One afternoon we went for a walk in the woods. After a while, we stopped talking. The leaves were dry and loud under our feet. Our silence was louder than our words.

"I'm scared," Jenny finally said, in a small voice.

"Scared of what?" I asked.

"I'm scared I can't stop. Like I'm on this path and I can't stop. I'm out of control. I'll have this baby, drop out of school, be a pathetic mother, get sick like my mother, raise a little girl like me. I'm really scared, Molly." She pulled off the path and rested her young woman-face into her hands and wept. That was the first time Jenny had revealed to me how afraid she was. It was the first time I had ever seen her cry.

I didn't have to get behind the wheel of that car. I got caught up in the fact that everyone else there would, and I would some-how let them down if I didn't, too. I risked my life because I was worried about being seen as "less than" or "chicken." I risked the future of my own children's well-being because of twenty-five people who didn't really care whether I did it or not, though I was sure they did. And once I'd started, I wanted to stop but I couldn't.

I'm forty-one years old and I'm in the business of teaching girls to stand up for themselves. That night at the speedway, I didn't do it.

Not even close.

I am no different than sweet Jenny who was influenced for whatever reason to have sex with someone when she didn't want to—not really, anyway. She gave up her little-girl life for that one immediate need to give in to the expectation of someone else.

She gave in. I gave in.

When I pulled the car over and the instructor came back and asked if I'd had fun, I thought about it for a minute and shook my head no. He didn't expect that for an answer. He asked if there was anything he could have done to make the experience more enjoyable. I couldn't think of it then.

But if he were to ask me that question again I might say, "How about a long walk in the woods, *first*?"

Jenny's lesson: Can you imagine the power of my actions if I had decided *not* to drive? The message I would have given to the people who really care about me, the message that I would have given to Hank and Helen, that they are more important than anything or anybody in this world, and that I would risk my life only to protect theirs—and for no other reason?

More important, what about the message I would have given to myself? Of standing up for what I believe is right, honorable, and true to my heart?

Can you begin to imagine the power of a little girl who decides that smoking isn't for her? Imagine the power of a little girl who cares for her body too much to entertain the idea of having sex before her spirit wants to? Imagine the power of a little girl who isn't afraid to tell you how she feels, the power of a little girl who believes in herself regardless of what others think or expect? Just imagine what we can learn from a little girl like that.

Now imagine a world full of little girls like that. Imagine your daughter being one of those.

What I learned from Jenny: Don't expect from my children what I don't expect from myself.

BLYTHE'S STORY

When I think about Blythe, I chuckle. She's funny. She's always a little scattered, a little messy, and very uninhibited. Blythe is in third grade. She makes her best effort to fit into the current clothing trend but is always just a bit off. (I can really relate to her on the whole fashion thing!)

Blythe is in Girls on the Run.

She was born prematurely—she was dangerously tiny at birth. She suffered numerous strokes in her mother's womb and had several more when she was born. The trauma left her mildly paralyzed on one side of her body. The slightest hint of a limp followed her with each step, as one leg lagged behind the other.

Blythe was thrilled to be in Girls on the Run. The noncompetitive and girl-friendly approach fit her like a custom-made suit. She was welcomed, accepted, and celebrated not in spite of her medical story but because of it!

May 4 was a big day that year for our Charlotte Girls on the Run participants. The Girls on the Run 5K race is held in a historic area of the city, where cherry blossoms and oak trees release so much pollen, you have to wash your windshield before heading to work in the morning. The dogwoods are in full bloom and their pink blossoms flow through the gutters of the city streets. The culmination of the girls' hard work would be celebrated on this day with the 5K run/walk that highlights what they've accomplished over the twelve-week program period.

Blythe was thrilled. The unseasonably cool temperature and torrential rains did not stop her from coming. She was one of 450 girls who cast aside any misgivings about the weather and came to run with their friends.

The course is three miles, composed of three one-mile loops. This way the girls can pass by the finish line crowd three times and receive triple the cheers, high-fives, and smiles from onlookers and fans. Blythe, in her characteristic "waddle," passed by me, wearing a smile on her face that reflected the spirit welling up inside her. That smile was contagious, spreading across the faces of the bystanders like the river of rain that poured down on them.

On the last lap, after all the other 450 participants had completed the race, there came Blythe up the last hill. I first saw the top of her head—her blond hair plastered to her scalp—next the glasses, and then the smile. Exuberant, joyous, and completely unleashed, her smile pulled her up that hill and right through the tape we had stretched across the finish line.

Her friends had gathered at the finish line to cheer on their wacky friend and they all did a "Blythe dance" when she was done. I was on my way in to the recreation center where the wrap-up ceremonies were going to take place when I felt a persistent tug on the back of my drenched sweatshirt.

It was Blythe. Her glasses were completely fogged up. Her bangs created rivulets of water down her face. And that smile—beautiful!

I chuckled. "What is it, honey?"

"Molly," she said between breaths, her little chest heaving in and out. "I just thought you might like to know. I feel the best about myself right now, that I ever have."

I looked at her and replied with the knowing that only comes from that intuitive, internal voice, "You know what, Blythe? I do, too." We held hands and walked into the rec center together.

Blythe's lesson: Feeling good about what we do, our accomplishments, and who we are has in many instances been labeled as cocky or conceited. But acknowledging our sense of worth, as Blythe did, is healthy.

Helen is still at the age where she constantly demands, "Mommy, look. Mommy, look. Mommy, *look* at me. Look at what I can do." She will then hang on the monkey bars or come down the slide at full speed. I will run to her, take her hands in mine, and ask her, "Helen, how does doing those wonderful things make you feel?"

And she will reply in the most unabashed voice, "I feel goooooooooooood!!"

Helen takes responsibility for her own worth. She says out loud that she feels good and she has done something extraordinary. She doesn't need my praises (although I give them to her frequently). She can praise herself. She can nourish that internal voice inside of her that knows she is worthwhile simply because she "is." She doesn't have to work for it, climb high mountains, or win races. There are no strings attached. She *is*; therefore, she is worthwhile.

The older I get, the better I am at shutting off the negative tapes in my brain and inserting more positive messages there. I don't look to others to nourish my self-worth as frequently as

I used to. When I humbly accept the gift of my own self-worth, I help others do the same.

What I learned from Blythe: Teach self-acceptance and self-love by living them.

SIERRA'S STORY

Sometimes Sierra lives with her father. And sometimes she lives with her grandmother. Sierra is very angry most of the time. Her brows are always furrowed—two deep trenches between two deep-brown eyes. Her hands are usually in fists—carried like block weights at the end of two very muscular, strong arms. When she walks her arms don't swing, they pump—like pistons emitting an energy that is both aggressive and intimidating. Sierra is in fifth grade.

And in Girls on the Run.

Her grandmother signed her up for the program. "Mamaw" is a strong Christian woman who has already raised four of her grandbabies. Her seventy-year-old body is tired and wizened. Her life is full—too full. Shuffling between two jobs, four grandchildren, and no sleep, Mamaw was doing the best she could. Sierra was in many ways responsible for her own upbringing. Yes, Mamaw had done the best she could, but now Sierra was in trouble. Her schoolwork was failing, she often came to school dirty, and she was always angry. With frequent altercations on the bus with peers and in the classroom with teachers, the girl was spiraling down fast.

Sierra was angry at Girls on the Run, too. But, mysteriously, she kept coming back. Unfortunately, her negative attitude was beginning to bring some of the other girls down. "This is stupid," she would utter with disgust at the mere mention of an activity.

I couldn't let it continue. I wanted to forget about it, pretend that her negative attitude wasn't there, but I just couldn't let it dampen the experience of all of the other girls. So I scheduled a meeting with her, her principal, and me.

And I learned something that to this day I never take for granted. Sierra didn't know what respect looked like. She didn't know what it meant to look someone in the eye. She had never had that kind of direct connect with any family members.

So for two hours she and I retired to the library. We settled into two beanbag chairs, our bare feet rubbing the old shag carpet under us. That afternoon, I taught her how to look someone in the eye. How to stand up tall when she walks. I taught her how to relax her shoulders and how to smile when spoken to. This was all very new to her and a world that no one ever told her existed. We wrote out a contract: She promised to try to perform these simple acts of respect at Girls on the Run. We outlined precisely what her rewards would be when she performed them. We also wrote out the consequences of any severe negative behaviors—clearly and succinctly, so there would be no surprises.

That week, her grandma died. Sierra didn't come back to Girls on the Run. She moved to another city to live with her daddy. I've often wondered what impact our two hours in the library had on her—whether she carried our list in her pocket, or whether she tossed it out with her move from the familiar to the unknown.

Sierra's lesson: I could have given up. I could have let her negative attitude influence the experience of all the other girls. But I knew that if her attitude was affecting me, it was definitely affecting other people in her life.

And so, instead of holding on to the I-can't-do-anything-about-this attitude she lived, I decided to do something. I believed in her extraordinariness. I believed in the power of positivism and decided to slow down long enough to show it to her.

I want to believe that she was influenced on some level by our encounter that afternoon in the library. I want to believe that a small seed was planted that day—a seed that will grow quietly in her soul and blossom one day, perhaps on a run one dramatic stormy July evening. I want to believe in the power of *her* extraordinariness.

What I learned from Sierra: Expect the extraordinary—from yourself and your children.

BRITNEY'S STORY:

This week marks the first anniversary of my mother's death. She would have been seventy-nine years old this Friday. Moments before I had gone to Girls on the Run, I had e-mailed one of my most intimate friends. "My mother's birthday is this week. I really miss her touch, the way she would push aside the strands of stray hair from my eyes, really embrace me, and tell me that 'everything's going to be okay.' "

Thirteen bright and enthusiastic girls anxiously awaited their first day of Girls on the Run. I walked up to them, full of anticipation, knowing the depth of relationship about to blossom. Six years ago, I walked up to thirteen little girls at this same location—nervous and unsure but convinced that something holy was about to occur. Many of the thirteen today are younger sisters of that inaugural class. One of those was an innocent and wide-eyed Britney. "I recognize you," I said. "I know your sister April."

"How did you know she was my sister?" she asked.

"You look just like her, only you are *you*." Britney smiled at me and skipped ahead to join the girls as they jostled for a place in our first circle as Girls on the Run.

Britney is a lot like her sister was. She appeared unfocused—somewhat disconnected from herself, with a strange, detached smile resting on her face the whole hour. It was as if the smile reflected something other than happiness, as if it didn't really match the true emotion underneath. Her big sister had been like that. April used to walk next to me—as close as she possibly could without actually getting in the way—always helpful, and always with that smile, which was sorrowful at best.

It was the fall of 1996. April's mother called me. "I'm going to the hospital for a few days. I just can't shake this depression that's eating me up inside. I wanted you to know because April feels a real connect with you. And while I'm completely useless as her mother right now, I need others who can stand in to support her." "Of course I'll support her," I replied. "But is there anything I can do for you?" I was totally honored that she felt safe enough with me to share such vulnerability. "No," she cried. "There's nothing you can do. There's nothing anyone can do."

Listening to the desperation in her voice, the crying out, I wanted to hold this woman—this mother—stroke her hair, embrace her, lift the guilt of the world from her shoulders, and tell her that everything would be all right. I wanted to mother her, to love her and lift her up as I did her daughter. "There is nothing you can do," she told me.

April continued to come to Girls on the Run—brought there by her grandmother, babysitters, and occasionally her father. Her mother was in the hospital for weeks.

Last March, I was at the Y. Seated on a couch in the ladies' locker room was April and Britney's mom. "I'm working out again now," she said. "I'm trying to quit smoking but having a hard time with that one." She smiled that detached smile, as if she knew this was the point in the conversation when she was *supposed* to smile—or feel something like happiness—but it was only an act, and I knew it. "I'm divorced and getting on with my life," she said. I sat down next to her, placed my hand on her shoulder, and told her how strong she was and how good it was to see her taking care of herself. Her eyes looked deeply into mine, as if begging my soul to make it so, to make her strong. She was hungry to feel that strength but she did not really feel it. "Tell April hey, would ya?" I asked her. "Sure, my little April is in eighth grade this year."

I went for my daily run, did my grocery shopping and went to work, picked up my kids, squeezed them tight, kissed them on their cheeks, and cooked dinner. Another ordinary day in March.

This week in Girls on the Run the girls were lined up side by side. One of the Getting to Know Each Other exercises has the girls play a game called I Like Relay. The coach shouts, "If you like chocolate-chip cookies, take off," and all those little girls who love chocolate-chip cookies fly toward the assistant coach standing thirty yards down the field. "If you think school is fun, take off." All but two ran. "If your parents are divorced, take off." Three girls took off.

Britney was one of those who ran on this one. When she returned to her spot, she said, "My parents were divorced before my mom died."

I looked at this beautiful third grader with the detached smile. "Your mom died. I'm so sorry, Britney." I took her hands, looked deep into her eyes, and for that moment the rest of the little girls dropped back into space. "Talk to me, what happened?"

"Last March, she suffocated, in her bed." I felt the silence of the moment sieve out all the other distractions—girls laughing at one another, holding hands, and talking about the day's events.

I flashed back to my conversation with Britney's mother at the Y a year earlier and wondered about the true circumstances of her death. I held one of Britney's hands, brushed aside the strands of hair from her eyes, hugged her tight, and told her, "Honey, everything's going to be okay."

Britney's lesson: Although I couldn't save Britney's mother, I can save her. The magnitude of my impact is *that* great. In instances like these, it comes down to actually saving lives. My job is to commit myself to living as fully as I can outside of it as an example to all the Aprils and Britneys out there who need that kind of role model. I do know that I can mother them and push the strands of hair out of their eyes so that they can see better the world we are creating for them, a world open and willing to love them just as they are. I do know that I can live my life fully assured that "everything is going to be okay."

And, by doing so, assure *them* of it.

My mother would be seventy-nine years old this week. How odd that my request for her touch, her embrace, her words of "everything will be okay" came to me, and how miraculous that they then came *from* me to a nine-year-old girl who had also lost her mother—and yearned for the very same thing.

What I learned from Britney: Give away what you desire and it will return tenfold.

HELEN'S STORY

Helen is only three—but I have come to expect nothing short of genius from her.

She is very independent and strong-willed, two things I

wish for any girl and yet, at times, these strengths of character can be a real challenge to a mother. Helen can now plop into her car seat and buckle it herself, an action in which she takes *great* pride.

Several months ago, on a cheery Monday morning, we climbed into the car—I, into the front seat and she, independently, into her car seat in the back. She snapped herself in and off we went. Several yards down the driveway I hear her sweet, petite voice. "Mommy, I'm hurting my nuts," she said calmly.

Trying to hold back the chuckle, I said, "Honey you aren't hurting your nuts." (Hank had only the day before referred to his own private parts as nuts. I was sure she was comparing her privates to his.) And then, as all wise and knowledgeable moms do, I thought to myself, *What a great opportunity to talk a little bit about the differences between boys and girls.* So I launched into a solid five minutes about how she did not have nuts and that, as a matter of fact, "nuts" isn't really a good word for those things. They are called testicles and only boys have them. There are two of them and they are located directly behind the . . . blah, blah, blah.

After my five-minute biology lesson, I looked in my rearview mirror and into the face of the most puzzled three-year-old I had ever seen. Her eyebrows were furrowed and her nose was scrunched as if to say, *Motherrrrrrrrr, why are you telling me this?* My biological moment sounded like nothing more to her than the hollow voice of Charlie Brown's teacher in all the Peanuts cartoons.

Several more minutes down the road, I heard, in a voice similar to the possessed voice of Linda Blair in *The Exorcist*, "MOMMY, I'M HURTING MY NUTS!!" I expected to see her head turn a full 360 degrees.

I pulled the car over at the first available opportunity, ran around to the back door, and examined the situation. Maybe she had somehow "snapped" herself with her car seat buckle—or, worse yet, really, *really* hurt herself where, if she had *had* nuts, her nuts would have been. "Honey, are you okay?" She squirmed for less than ten seconds, reached down under the right cheek of her buttocks and pulled out a handful of acorns!

Now I'm waiting for a phone call from the day care center: "Ms. Barker, your daughter did the strangest thing today. She picked up an acorn and with delight exclaimed, 'Look everybody, a testicle!' "

Helen's lesson: Sometimes a nut is just a nut. Sometimes adults tell too much. Sometimes we speak before really listening to our children. Sometimes we think we know what our kids are talking about and we don't really have any clue. Sometimes our children are so genuinely funny, it's impossible to not laugh. Sometimes we need to not take ourselves so darn seriously.

What I learned from Helen: Seek first to understand and then be understood—*and* make sure to laugh a lot in the process.

She is in there. The queen is strong, powerful, and waiting for permission to reveal herself. I know this. I have seen her and she is coming.

So, to review:

1. Celebrate your daughter's body;
2. Celebrate your daughter's spirit;
3. Celebrate your daughter's voice;
4. Celebrate your daughter's gifts;
5. Celebrate the joys of parenthood;
6. Celebrate the magic of your daughter's imagination;

7. Try to seek the positive in all people and circumstances;

8. Don't expect from your children what you don't expect from yourself;

9. Teach self-acceptance and self-love by living them;

10. Expect the extraordinary—from yourself and your children;

11. Give away what you desire and it will return tenfold;

12. Seek first to understand and then be understood—*and* make sure to laugh a lot in the process.

One day last week, I went running through downtown Charlotte with nothing on but a jogbra and running shorts. What freedom to let my body show, my highlighted hair flow behind me. I spit somewhere on that run, had sweat pouring down my back, and jaywalked on East Boulevard. I disregarded the traffic light at Kenilworth, stopped for water at a gas station, and used the restroom at the park.

I spent most of that time thinking about where I was going to dinner, what to buy my daughter for her birthday, and how to get my son to do his homework. Next week Helen will be four. We plan to go to La-tea-da's for a tea party with her friends. We will dress up in totally goofy big hats, have tea, and pretend to be ladies.

And somewhere right now, right this minute, while I'm writing this, a young woman lies silent, starving herself to be beautiful and invisible; a young girl is having sex so her boyfriend will love her; a young mother is selling her pregnant body so she can get her next heroin kick; a little girl thinks she isn't worth anything because she is fat; a mother hides her liquor but can't hide the odor of it on her breath or the shame of it in her soul when her daughter comes home from school; a woman stays in an abusive situation while her daughter wonders why; and an eleven-year-old girl tries her first cigarette.

My desire to celebrate my children and all the girls with whom I come into contact is stronger than it ever has been. We've got to start somewhere. We've got to take back our voices, our bodies, our spirits.

Next week, I will celebrate my daughter's birthday. She will play dress-up in frills and a hat and hold a teacup with her pinky finger extended. We will talk to her stuffed animals, giggle for no reason, and eat cake.

Today, somewhere, a girl cries in shame—for no real reason.

I want to know her. I want to get to know her, celebrate her, see her eyes. I want to kiss her cheek, dance with her in the sunshine, lift her up, and celebrate all the girl that she is and the woman she will be. I want her to know that she is beautiful, strong, and powerful.

Our jobs—yours and mine—are to give girls back their bodies, their voices, and their spirits. To take them back from the negative stereotypes and messages in the media. To take them back from the *should* and *ought to* people. To put their uniqueness, their individuality, their girlness at the core of all we do for them and with them. To provide as many opportunities as possible for our girls to experience genuine acceptance of themselves, just as they are.

And what continually comes back to haunt me in all of my work with girls—and even more so as the mother of one—is this: I cannot give away what I do not already have.

I cannot dance with her until I get the strength to push free the doors and flee the Girl Box.

I cannot lift her up into the sunshine until I am willing to step out from the darkness of the Girl Box.

I cannot look into her eyes and see the strength there

until I am willing to look inward and see the strength that lies within me.

Your body is your body—love it.

Your voice is your voice—use it.

Your spirit is your spirit—celebrate it.

And prepare to meet the queen.

FOUR

IN THE CARDS

The precepts of the Girls on the Run program were based on the work of several fine psychological studies. I learned of these while working toward my masters in social work at the University of North Carolina at Chapel Hill and while working at the Drug Education Center in Charlotte.

An understanding of these studies (in very simple, lay terms), I think, will enhance your understanding of this text AND better serve you and your "girl" while you try to navigate the waters of girlhood, teenhood, and adulthood. While I am not an analytical person, I am very interested in self-improvement, so hang in there with me. The following information will probably not come as a surprise but will more than likely inspire you, as it did me, to do something for your daughter and all of the other girls out there that crave a positive frame of reference.

INSTILLING RESILIENCY

In his text, *Regaining Excellence in Education,* Mario Fantini discusses three elements that increase a child's likelihood of maintaining his or her self-esteem through the often turbulent times of adolescent development.

Those three key elements are:

One: **A secure sense of identity and a deep understanding of her values.** Girls need to know what they stand for and what is meaningful to them. They need to understand why they behave in the ways that they do. They need to make the correlation between their behavior and the value beneath the surface of it. They need to declare, for themselves, what is important.

Two: **A feeling of connectedness.** A girl needs to feel a part of something greater than herself. She needs to feel connected with a group of individuals that care about her, love her, and nourish her soul. She needs to feel a bond with others who share in her values, support her, and lift her up when she needs encouragement. She may find this sense of connectedness through her family, her religious affiliation and her peers, clubs at school, or sports teams.

Three: **A feeling of empowerment.** Girls today often feel as if decisions are made for them. Parents, in an effort to instill values in their daughters, often confuse instilling those values with declaring those values for their daughter: "We are Smiths, and Smiths don't believe in _____." A young girl needs opportunities to come to her own conclusions, make her own decisions, and experience some sense of empowerment in the decisions that she makes. She needs to feel that she can positively affect the world in which she lives.

Girls on the Run makes every effort to provide these opportunities to its participants. This text, too, will take you through the process of values clarification, partnership building, and increasing your sense of empowerment.

First, let's take a minute and look at some concrete ways you can use the research to enhance your girl's well-being.

One: **Values clarification.** What is a value? In a nutshell, think of things—ideas and concepts—that are valuable to you. Values that we discuss in Girls on the Run are respect for others, respect for oneself, self-discipline, humility, education, honesty, and acceptance, to name a few. Generally at the core of all things we hold to be valuable is a concept that captures the essence of the *thing* we value.

For example, consider the person who values family. While family is something she expresses as a value she holds deeply in her heart, the deeper values that family represents to her are love, connectedness, and respect.

Now, consider the little girl who comes from a home where family is not a positive influence in her life. While she may not value the concept of family, she may embrace the values that family represents to others for whom it *is* a positive influence— again, love, respect, connectedness. Her expression of these core values may manifest itself when she says that friends are valuable to her.

So when your child expresses something as important to her, question her a little more deeply and see if you can't get to the core of *why* that thing is valuable to her. Perhaps her incessant demand for you to brush and style her hair each morning has nothing to do with the way she looks and more to do with the time she shares with you in doing so. Her love for you and your attention are important to her. This will further enhance your relationship—because as you learn more about what is valuable to her, you can find a variety of ways to reinforce those values that are positive for her.

Getting your girl to identify the core value behind her behaviors and beliefs can be a challenge. I personally struggle at times with determining what is the motivating value behind some of my actions. Why am I polite? Because I value respect for others. Why do I exercise? Because I have self-respect. Why do I make a gratitude list at the conclusion of each day? Because I value gratitude.

Being an active listener is crucial to helping your girl determine the values at the core of her belief system. Active listening takes time and is deliberate. Active listening requires mastery over the following three concepts: listening for content; listening for feelings; and listening for value.

When actively listening to your girl (or anyone for that matter), your goal is not to offer advice (unless she asks for it), judge, or take inventory of the content of what is being said. Your goal is to walk your girl through her *own* thought processes—from the experience she describes to the core value represented by that experience.

While actively listening, turn off your cell phone, shut off any watch alarms, turn off the television—basically shut down any external noise (metaphorically speaking as well).

An example of a good listening mother might include the following dialogue.

GIRL *(age ten):* Mom, you wouldn't believe what happened today. During recess all of the boys started chasing Frances. She had on a shirt that had a zipper down the front and they were pretending, as they chased her, to grab the zipper and unzip it. Some of the boys were chasing her and popping her bra strap. They weren't really interested in chasing me. I couldn't believe Frances let them do that. She was laughing about it and seemed to think it was funny. I didn't think it was funny at all.

MOM (listening for content, paraphrasing, interjecting an uh-uh every once in a while, making good eye contact): So today during recess, some of the boys were chasing Frances and pretending to unzip her shirt and were popping her bra strap. On the other hand, they weren't chasing you. You thought it wasn't funny—but Frances seemed to be almost enjoying it. Right?

GIRL: Yeah. I didn't understand what all the fun was about it. As a matter of fact, I felt left out.

MOM (listening for feelings): Honey, I'm hearing that you felt left out, and guessing you were maybe even a little sad. You haven't started wearing a bra yet, and while Frances needs one—well, she is maturing faster than you—I know sometimes that you feel not as popular as her because of it. You might have even been feeling a little jealous of her. Does that sound like what you were feeling?

GIRL: Yes. I hate the way I'm maturing so much slower than the other girls, and the way the boys give Frances all the attention just because she has bigger boobs than I do.

MOM (listening for value): You know what I find absolutely amazing about you? You are so aware of what you are feeling. It sounds to me like you want to be liked for who you are, not what you look like or the size of your breasts. Am I right about that? Like maybe what is most important about a person is what makes her beautiful from the inside and not from the outside?

GIRL: Well, now that you put it that way—you're right.

MOM (affirming the positive value): I think it's wonderful that you think like that. That is a very noble value that you possess. Let's think of some ways that you can honor that value with yourself and even with Frances.

And from this can evolve a wonderful dialogue about how to stand up to peer pressure and hold true to the values we possess.

It's never too early to begin to assist your girl in clarifying her values—sometime during second and third grade she is able to grasp more abstract concepts, such as acceptance, nondiscrimination, self-love, and internal beauty. Every moment is a teachable moment. Explain to her the value behind your own actions: "Today, honey, I'm returning the CD I borrowed from Susan, because I respect her and need to respect her possessions." Or: "I'm cleaning up my room before I leave the house so that when I come home at the end of the day, I can relax and enjoy time with you. I'm working on being more self-disciplined." Or: "Let's call Dori and tell her how thankful we are that she is our friend. You know, I really value being grateful for all the wonderful things I have." A quick statement like this doesn't take much time but helps your girl understand the motive behind your actions.

Two: **Connectedness.** Third and fourth grade is a magical time in the parent-daughter, mentor-mentee, adult-child relationship. While the child is beginning to build strong ties to her peer group, she is still willing to listen to the adults in her life. It is a very critical time in assisting your girl as she maneuvers the waters of those first cliques, arguments with friends, and the whole drive to be popular.

While she is still in this willing-to-listen stage of her development, consider getting her involved in some type of extracurricular activity that focuses on healthy, positive values.

Perhaps affiliate her with a religious group that you can support or in which you are actively involved. Sports are another avenue where she is likely to encounter many positive experiences and values that enhance her self-esteem. This is one of the primary purposes of Girls on the Run. Is she musically inclined? Perhaps she would like to study a musical instrument. Does she sing? Instead of private lessons, you might consider group lessons where she can develop a feeling of connectedness with other young musicians.

Create a "swinging door" atmosphere in your home to provide a place where her friends are welcome. See whom your girl invites over. You can better understand who her peers are if you leave your door open for all to enter. You can watch her as she interacts with her friends. Should she have a friend who constantly provides conflict in her life, you will know it and be able to discuss the core values at the heart of friendship and determine if these values are being exhibited in her relationship with this person. If she doesn't embrace the values of a healthy friendship now, it will be more challenging to limit her contact with unhealthy peers once she enters middle and high school.

Establish a group where other mothers and daughters (including stepmothers and -daughters), mentors and mentees, aunts and nieces get together on a regular basis. Form a book club. Develop friendships with the parents of your girl's friends. This way you can share thoughts, observations, and concerns with other parents who also see your girl on a regular basis.

My son is in second grade. In his eyes, I am still pretty cool. Every afternoon, without fail, I pick him up at his after-school enrichment program and stay for at least a good thirty minutes, cutting up with his friends and him. They all call me Miss Molly and they truly love when I walk in that door. I'm fun and engaging and I'm sincerely interested in what they are saying and doing. My son is proud to call me his mother. I realize that his comfort with my presence among his peers will likely be short-lived. But I want to believe that if I develop a relationship with his friends now, the relationships will remain as we all grow older.

In a nutshell, be a directive parent in determining your child's peer groups at an early age. If you combine this kind of direction with discussion around the value of healthy friendships, you will know that you are providing them with the necessary tools to seek out healthy, fulfilling relationships in the future.

Three: **Empowerment.** Many children today don't feel like they have much say in the direction in which their lives are headed. It feels good to make a decision and have the outcome of your decision prove beneficial. My four-year-old daughter gets to make a decision every morning. "Helen, do you want Cheerios or cornflakes?" Some days she picks cornflakes, other days it's Cheerios. Whichever she chooses she has jump-started her day by making a decision that proves beneficial to her. She is empowered. She feels good about the decision she made, has bought into the outcome, and eats up her whole bowl of cereal without complaint.

The real world isn't quite so simple. Choices that kids are forced to make nowadays are varied and often frightening. Do I smoke or not smoke? Do I drink alcohol or pass it up? Do I have intercourse or do I wait until I am older? I feel a powerful pain in my heart when I consider the many negative influences that could possibly distract my children as they grow up. So while I might like to remove those options from her list, I must also realize that every time my daughter chooses an option—as I did in my youth and even now—there is a wealth of knowledge and personal growth that comes with each choice.

The *greatest* gift I can give my own children is the power of their own decisions. With every decision comes a consequence and at the core of each decision made is a central value. I pray for my daughter to have the strength to handle whatever consequences her decisions may bring.

As I go through life, am *I* honoring my core values or am I chipping away at my self-worth by acting in a way that sabotages my core values? Getting up every day is a decision. Going to school every day is a decision. Show your girl that she is powerful by pointing out the hundreds of decisions she makes every day.

Take *every* opportunity you have to support your girl's making healthy decisions. Acknowledge the positive results of healthy decisions. Help her see that every move she makes is a decision. "Honey, I am so proud of you for doing your homework right off the bat, when you got home. You didn't have to, but you did. Way to go! Obviously you value education and following through on commitments you make. I am truly impressed."

Just two nights ago my daughter decided to sleep in her brother's room. Hank has a bunk bed. Helen was on the top bunk and Hank was on the bottom. Helen started to get scared in the new environment of Hank's room. I heard Hank talking his little sister through the fear, helping her acknowledge it but then taking her to a place of comfort by telling her a familiar bedtime story about Kermoodgie the dragon that I used to tell when they were little. The next morning when Hank came down, sleepy-eyed and groggy, I wrapped him up in my arms and told him how amazing he was. "Hank, you are, without question, one of the most compassionate little boys I have ever known. I overheard what you did last night to help out your little sister. You didn't have to do that, but you did. You made a decision, honey, to help her out. Obviously, you love her very much and she loves you very much. Thank you for being such a good big brother." Well, by the time I was through with him he had a smile across his face and a spark in his eye. He felt good about his decision to help out his little sister.

Having a positive attitude is a decision. Helen and Hank will at times be screeching at each other in the backseat of my car. I will calmly (at first, or if it's not 5 P.M.) ask them to "change your attitude, please." Helen is quicker to make the transition and then Hank will follow suit. While having a positive attitude seems like a "should" kind of behavior, it really isn't—it's a choice. As often as I can, I acknowledge the positive decisions they make at each and every turn of their day. Having a positive attitude is one of those. I don't want to ever take their decisions for granted.

Another, more visible way to show your children the power of their own decisions is to give them the opportunity to impact their community. The last several weeks of the Girls on the Run program are designed to assist the girls through the development, design, and implementation of a community project. Why don't you and your girl consider doing a community project together? While this element is not a formal part of this text, I highly recommend that you determine a way for you and your girl to give back. Set aside one hour to determine what she and you could do to positively influence the town in which you live. Maybe you can pick up trash throughout your neighborhood. Consider serving up lunch on Thanksgiving Day at a homeless shelter. Ask your friends for used toys and games and take them down to the battered women's shelter. Get as creative as you want. Plant a garden in an urban neighborhood. Write letters to all U.S. senators about a particular political issue that concerns you.

One of the most powerful community projects ever implemented by a group of Girls on the Run was also one of the simplest. Twenty little girls made forty paper flowers and attached the following message to each one: "I give you a flower, to brighten your day, the beauty of it to lighten your way. A world of love is what we can achieve, if you place it on the car next to you as you leave." They randomly placed the flowers on the windshields of cars around the YMCA parking lot. Forty flowers were circulating around that neighborhood within minutes. Something as simple as a flower formed by the hands of a very special child affected hundreds of people throughout that city for weeks to come. So don't overdo it. Keep it simple and realize your power to influence your world!

THE BARKER TAKE ON REALITY THERAPY

I have long been a huge fan of William Glasser. When I was a cross-country coach, the mother of one of my runners handed me the book *Reality Therapy*. I was very interested in the works of William Glasser from that point on. In a nutshell, Glasser's Reality Therapy acknowledges that we behave in certain ways as the result of two very powerful motives: to be loved and to feel worthwhile. I can remember thinking, "That's it. He's got it. Of *course* that's why we behave the way we do." Glasser explained that all human behavior could be traced back to these two inherent needs, to be loved and to feel worthwhile.

Years later I was making a presentation to a large group about the prevention of eating disorders. I was launching into my explanation of Reality Therapy when I inadvertently switched the phrase from "to be loved and to feel worthwhile" to "to feel love and be worthwhile." I paused for a minute, prepared to correct myself, when it struck me. "No, *that's* it. That's what I want to motivate me."

So take a minute and acknowledge the powerful difference in the placement of those two words, *feel* and *be*. As women, we have been raised to consider being loved as one of our goals in life. We want to be loved by our children, by our spouses or partners, by our colleagues—we want to be loved by everyone and everybody. While this is absolutely impossible, many women spend their entire lives seeking to *be loved*. Consider the woman who thinks that changing the shape of her body through surgical manipulations will bring her love, or the teenage girl who has sex—even though she would prefer not to—so that "he will love me." What about the eleven-year-old who smokes her first cigarette so "my friends will love me." Our entire socialization process gives us a false sense of control that we can somehow affect others' loving us by how we change ourselves.

This false perception is the core value of all Girl Box inhabitants. We perform life as opposed to experiencing it. We will alter our bodies, our hair color (I still haven't let go of that one!), our lifestyles, our beliefs, our morals, our *selves* to be loved by someone—anyone. Advertising companies have taken advantage of our belief in this false concept and run with it. Our teeth need to be whiter, our bodies need to be thinner or buffer or bigger-busted and smaller-butted, our houses have to be spick-and-span, our dishes have to be shinier, our clothes have to have certain labels, our children have to behave this way or that, our skin needs to be wrinkle free, and heaven forbid we have cellulite! We are never—*never*—good enough, pretty enough, slim enough, rich enough, or perfect enough, and the implication in this way of thinking is that once we manage to get "good enough" (which is impossible according to these standards), we will be loved.

If our motivation is to *feel* love, the Girl Box magically slips away. We can climb right out of that box and be on our peaceful, content, and joyous way. Feeling love gives me back my body, my *self*, my hair, my *life*. If my motive is to feel love, I become an active participant in life. I begin to *experience* love as opposed to waiting for someone else to love me.

This is where things get tough. The best way to teach our children this philosophical change is to live it. We can bring it to their consciousness through discussion, but I am convinced that the best way of teaching how to feel love is to feel love in all that we do, to practice the behaviors that feeling love evokes in our interactions with our kids.

How does feeling love play itself out in a woman's life? **First we learn to love ourselves.** This includes accepting our bodies. We realize that love—deep, authentic love—has little to do with the size of our breasts or the shape of our butts. Ironically, we become more beautiful to those around us when we begin to love ourselves. Self-love is the best cosmetic. Respecting our bodies, nurturing the physical self that houses the "who" in who we are, is a sign of self-love. We walk more confidently (yet with humility), become grateful for the marvelous things our bodies can do—as opposed to condemning them for what they can't do. We admire our form in the mirror and ask our daughters to do the same. I can say to my four-year-old, "Helen, look at your belly. You have the most beautiful belly I have ever seen. Look at that! Do you realize how absolutely beautiful that belly of yours is?" We can help our daughters celebrate their features—their unique body traits. Gaps in teeth, freckles on noses, scars on knees, birthmarks on bellies, bushy eyebrows, thin lips, curly hair—all are unique and thoroughly beautiful. Educate her early.

Another aspect of loving ourselves outside of the physical is **loving our strengths.** While I am a visionary person—full of ideas and wonder at all the day has to offer—I tend to be weak on the details of follow-through. But Elaine, who works in my office, is a whiz on details—hence we make a marvelous team. She celebrates her attention to detail in her work as I celebrate my attention to vision in mine. Celebrating our strengths means finding our passions in work and our relationships. A strength I have always possessed has been my athleticism. I celebrate that strength through running and, occasionally, racing. I love the sound of speed as it rushes through my ears, the sweat down my back, and the ground under my feet. Another strength I celebrate is my ability to connect with people. Through my own struggles with alcoholism, I realize that I am no better and no worse than anyone. I recognize that everyone has his/her story. I celebrate my strength to develop rapport easily in my work and in my personal relationships. Help your girl identify her strengths both in her character and her physical capabilities and look for as many occasions as possible to celebrate them.

Loving ourselves also means **loving and celebrating our sexuality**. We are sexual beings. To deny that part of our womanhood is to deny a huge part of who we are. There doesn't exist a more controversial, confusing, misunderstood issue in American feminist culture than our sexuality. I recently spoke at a conference on "Sexuality and the American Teen." Among America's top educators there is still confusion regarding what is the correct tack when discussing sexuality with young girls. At the center of the controversy rest our personal beliefs about the meaning of sex and the value we each place on it. While I can't define that for you, I can suggest that being sexual is part of human nature. And rather than shut down the sexual voice that resides inside you, allow it to flourish in a way that celebrates your spirit. Attach a value to it and then let your behavior follow suit. Help your girl understand and accept her sexual self. Be honest with her about it and keep the lines of communication open. A healthy attitude toward her sexual self will offer her many opportunities, which, as she matures into a wise woman, will allow her to feel love, celebrate her body, and simply have fun. Discuss the negative consequences of using sex as a tool to manipulate others. Acknowledge her sexual self when she begins to realize she has it and give her the freedom to express it in a way that expresses self-love, self-respect, and respect of others as opposed to a tool or weapon to get something (or someone) she wants. Imagine the mature strength of your daughter's character if she were able to talk to you about her sexual desires. You needn't be shocked by them; rather, recognize that they are normal and actually healthy. Like any other expression of self, help her see the importance of expressing her sexual self in a way that honors her spirit and the spirit of others.

Another detrimental result of the needing-to-be-loved philosophy of the Girl Box is the need to people please. People pleasing comes in many forms. People pleasers have a fear of confronting someone who has harmed them or is currently harming them.

Consider the college student who returns to her dorm room with her date and proceeds to "make out" with him. At some point the physical comfort she takes in his arms crosses over to a place of discomfort—but rather than speaking up for herself she goes ahead and has intercourse and regrets it after he leaves. A woman who is intentionally feeling love WILL stand up for herself for many reasons. First, she respects herself and her values. She isn't comfortable and lets her date know. Another element of feeling love rests in her love or respect for her date. To give in to the physical moment isn't a true representation of who she is and what she values—she is not being truthful with her date and is therefore not respecting him. If he argues against her desire to stop, he isn't respecting her and she doesn't continue the relationship.

Needing to be loved is actually a very selfish act. The focus rests on our needs and discounts our concern for the other person. We give the other person what they want—not because it is the altruistic and honorable thing to do, but because we want something in return.

As a parent, I struggle with kid pleasing more than any other piece of my relationship with my children. At 5 P.M. when I am totally exhausted, I may feel like becoming a lazy parent. Sometimes I do. "Okay, Hank," I say, "go ahead and have an ice-cream sandwich," when what I really want him to do is skip the ice cream and save space for a healthier dinner. But I'm tired and he knows it, and he gets his way. Instead of the work involved in saying no, I give in. It's not a healthy model of boundaries for him and I feel manipulated. We need to set boundaries with our kids. We can be their friends, but we also need to be the parent. Their persistent desire for more, more, more (they, too, are consumers that advertising hits in a big way) needs to be curtailed with a direct "no more" and end it right there. This is the loving thing to do. Raising them with no regard for personal boundaries isn't healthy—we may get into painful arguments or "Mom, I hate you" kinds of remarks, but they will be happier, healthier adults because we didn't people/kid please when they were young.

The other half of the Reality Therapy motive is to "feel worthwhile." My twist on that statement is to "*be* worthwhile." This again creates a powerful shift in the meaning of motive. The moment my children entered the world—actually, the moment they were conceived—they were worthwhile. They didn't need to *feel* worthwhile, perform any tricks, say please and thank you, smile at me—all they had to do was exist. We are worthwhile *because* we exist. To assume anything different is an insult to the higher power that resides in each of us. When we accept the fact that we simply are worthwhile, we treat ourselves with respect and, in turn, treat others with respect. We genuinely love ourselves and those around us. This acceptance of our "worthwhile-ness" takes us full circle back to the first premise that feeling love, as opposed to being loved, is the greater way. (Not always the easiest, however.)

Consider your girl. It's late in the day and she is behaving poorly. She is whining, arguing with her brother—she is basically pushing every last one of your buttons. Assuming that she is worthwhile, comments such as "You are a brat," or "You are stupid" or "You are driving me completely crazy" are meaningless. We can't be worthwhile *and* stupid *and* a brat. A better approach would be to acknowledge that her *behavior* is not appropriate. "Honey, your behavior is clearly not appropriate. The whining needs to stop. Until you can talk to me in a more respectful, pleasant tone, I will need you to go to time-out." Treat her with respect. Use time-out instead of physical discipline. Name-calling, screaming matches (although we've all done it and probably will in the future) are futile when it comes to assisting our girls in finding their own voice of self-discipline.

Another key to feeling love and being worthwhile is to acknowledge the intuitive voice that rests in each of us. Too often we listen to the voices of culture, socialization, and the media. Shutting down the noise of the outside world and listening to the rightness we hear inside is one way to acknowledge our worthwhile-ness. I have one or two very close friends with whom I will bounce off the words of my intuitive voice, and because I respect them I appreciate their feedback. But I generally try to shut out the stereotyping and negative voices screaming at me in the media—all those institutions that want to put me in the box. The occasions where I have *not* honored my intuitive voice and then "listened backward"—after the fact—I have discovered that the voice inside of me was truthful all along.

A question that is used in my house more than any other is: "What do you think about that?" or "How do you feel about that?" Instead of my telling my children the right and wrong way to think or feel, I let them voice their thoughts. When Helen jumps up joyously after a ride down the sliding board, I clap for her and ask "How do you feel?" She yells, "I feel *SUUUUUUUUPERRRRRRRRR!*" in her loudest voice. I tell her that I feel super watching her have fun and feel good. I want her to grow up listening to the golden truth of her own intuition—the "God voice" that rests inside.

THE WHOLE-PERSON CONCEPT

In the late '80s I was at the height of my competitive athletic performance. I had stopped drinking for a short period, what some clinicians call a dry drunk. I was physically very healthy. I was training for ironman triathlon events (2.4-mile swim, 112-mile bike ride, and 26.2-mile run) and working part-time. My life revolved around my sports life. I ate, drank, and breathed training. I might not have been drinking—but I was obsessive about my preparation for triathlons.

The finish results of my races proved that I was at my athletic peak. I was winning lots of races, qualifying for national-caliber events, and well known in triathlon circles.

What didn't show was my total lack of self-esteem—the never-ending message of "I'm not good enough" or "if only I had done this or that." I was never satisfied. I was stuffing away my emotions—outwardly I was a person who had it together, but I was crumbling on the inside.

I was a person living an unbalanced life. I was taking care of my physical needs and body, but was neglecting my emotions and mental health. Wellness is not about working out daily or eating only healthy foods. Total wellness takes into account our physical, emotional, social, mental, and spiritual health.

The Girls on the Run curriculum makes every effort to enhance these five facets of the blossoming girl-spirit. Consider these five "selves" when talking to your own girl. The lessons in this book attempt to support the emotional, social, physical, mental, and spiritual sides of both you and your girl.

An **emotionally healthy** person expresses a wide range of emotions. She is able to name her emotions and feel them fully. An emotionally healthy girl doesn't attempt to avoid any particular emotion. She doesn't try to run away from or cover up her anger, sorrow, frustrations, or fear. She doesn't show only the emotions that society considers positive (happiness, joy, peace, confidence). She doesn't deny herself her emotional voice.

Teach your girl that emotions are neither good nor bad. They simply are. It is the *behavior* stemming from those emotions that can be labeled productive or unproductive. For example, if a girl gets angry with her little sister for borrowing her clothes without asking and then hits her little sister, this behavior is inappropriate. The anger is perfectly normal and acceptable, but managing the anger through violence is not a healthy means of expressing it. Confronting her little sister by saying, "Susan, I feel angry when you borrow my clothes without asking, because it is disrespectful. I would like you to ask me in the future," is a more mature way to express her anger. (We will discuss this further in the following chapters.)

A **socially healthy** person has a good grasp on how to get along with others. She is a good listener, understands the importance of cooperation, doesn't gossip, attempts to keep a positive attitude, and maintains values that support her community, such as honesty, compassion, acceptance, and nondiscrimination. A socially healthy person responds to both internal and external stimuli in a way that asserts her own rights without infringing upon others'.

A **physically healthy** person recognizes the wonder in her own body. The expression "treat your body as a temple" reflects the attitude of a physically healthy person. A physically healthy person consciously acknowledges that without a healthy body, she can't live a healthy, full, productive life. Eating right, getting plenty of sleep, regular checkups, drinking plenty of water are, of course, *all* healthy ways to take care of our physical selves. But consider the less obvious. Celebrate the way your body moves through space when you walk. Carry yourself with confidence. Consider the beauty of your smile and the expression in your eyes. Love the shape of your body, the feminine curves of your frame, and the way your hands caress and nurture those you love.

Physical health is a frame of mind. How old would you be if you didn't have an age? Your body is earth's gift to you. Without it, you would not be able to enjoy the fruits of your spirit—in this lifetime at least. So, never condemn, speak negatively about, or harm your body. Your girl will watch you love your body and inevitably do the same.

Being **mentally healthy** is more difficult to acknowledge. Sometimes our own neuroses fool us into thinking that we are mentally healthy when in reality we are not. A mentally healthy person doesn't get stuck in repeating thoughts or behaviors that decrease his/her ability to function in society. Ironically, it's easier to determine when a person is NOT mentally healthy than when they are. A mentally healthy person tends to live a balanced life. Her life is not chaotic—it runs relatively smoothly. When a challenge comes along, she tackles it head-on: She deals with it, seeks to learn the lesson from it, and moves on.

Much of today's mental illness comes from individuals' trying to avoid something that is seen as negative or uncomfortable. We don't like delaying our gratification. We try to avoid confrontation, hard work, and disciplined behavior. The avoidance of these difficult tasks leads to our search for the quick fix—hence, many mentally ill people find solace in alcohol, drugs, eating disorders, sex, food addictions, work addictions, and relationship addictions. There is, in the life of a mentally disabled person, a sense of chaotic living. Decisions are made impulsively, finances may be in crisis and relationships in disarray. The mentally healthy person breathes deeply, tackles issues, and generally slows down the chaos of the immediate-gratification society.

Spiritual health is one of those pieces of daily living that is so individual, I can't possibly define it. What I know, for me, is in the theme that permeates this book, my life, and my relationships. Without a connection to or a belief in something—for me, that's a Higher Power—I lack purpose in my life. For years I sought worth and purpose in the hundreds of external distractions of our quick-fix world. Today, my drive to be spiritually healthy is at the core of who I am. My attempt to stay in constant contact with my Higher Power provides me with a purpose for living. I need to take care of all of the other parts of myself—my physical, emotional, mental, and social selves—so that I can fulfill my purpose.

Taking time to nourish my spiritual health provides me with so much gratitude for the world around me. Even the smallest insect has a purpose. I am no better, worse, or different than the blade of grass that sprouts up through the thick red clay in the glorious spring sun. This connection with something greater than myself provides me with purpose. I am a caregiver, not only of myself and my own children, but an exquisite instrument here to nourish *all* the children of the world and the lands upon which we live. Only through a concerted effort can I find spiritual health. It doesn't just rain down upon me. I have to push forth my tongue to taste the delicious wetness of it, take off the external world's distractions to feel the drops of it run down my skin. I have to slow down long enough to see it water love's roots in all living creatures.

Not too long ago I was meeting with Dr. Russell Pate. Russ is one of the finest exercise/physiology researchers in the country. He manages million-dollar research grants that evaluate exercise and healthy living programs for children and adults. We were talking about possible research opportunities for Girls on the Run. After much discussion, he asked me, "Molly—have you ever marketed your program? Have you ever developed a marketing plan or solicited folks to become directors in the states in which you now operate?" I told him that we have done absolutely none of that. I explained that the program has grown on its own—through word of mouth, mostly. Russ shook his head and said, "Now, there's your research project. It would be interesting to measure why the program has grown as it has—so quickly and so passionately all over the United States."

I chuckled for a minute and then followed up with the question "Can you evaluate God?"

As I look at the smiling faces and sparkling eyes of the girls in the program, the women who coach them, and the parents at the finish line there is no question that something very, very, VERY powerful is at work.

I have never seen the wind, but I know it exists. I can feel it on my skin and in my hair—I can see how it blows the leaves on the trees. So while I can't actually see the wind, I can easily see the result of it. I believe in the wind because I feel and see its influence on me and the world around me.

Believing in the presence of a Higher Power is like that for me. While I can't see the spirit directly, I *can* feel the love of it when my children touch my hand or smile at me. I can't protect my children from the scary things of the world or the possible negative consequences of their unhealthy decisions. What I can do is believe in the invisible wind that blows the trees and moves through my hair. I can have faith in a divine energy that will cradle them when they are afraid, teach them in painful moments, and lead them through a life of discovery, growth, and acceptance. My job as their parent, educator, and coach is to provide every opportunity that I can to connect with and increase their awareness of this divinity.

FIVE

MAKING THE MOST OF YOUR
CLIMBING-OUT-OF-THE–GIRL BOX EXPERIENCE

Now we get into the real nuts and bolts of preparing yourselves for the twenty lessons that follow in this chapter.

The lessons are based in large part on the many years of
work I have put into the Girls on the Run program. The idea is
to combine running or walking with lessons that teach both
you and your girl some actual life skills that will assist you in
breaking free of the Girl Box and the expectations placed on
you there. If you don't enjoy running, that's okay. I always tell
the girls they can hop, skip, jump, roll, cartwheel, *or* run. The
idea is to move your bodies just enough to physically push
yourselves a little bit outside of your comfort zone.

Running/walking is such a metaphor for our lives, in so
many ways. We have two choices in life: to go backward or forward. Standing still doesn't push us to grow, explore, and learn

about ourselves. What you and your girl(s) will learn about yourselves as you encourage your bodies to move forward, either by running or walking, will teach you many lessons about your strength of character and the depth of your spirit.

GETTING STARTED

First check your calendar. Make the lessons a priority. Set aside a time—preferably two days a week—where you and your girl(s) are completely focused on the lesson and one another. If you and your daughter(s) are doing this together, consider finding a friend to watch your other children. Go to a park or in the front yard. You can play the games anywhere there is some space to run and play; however, you will experience the most physical benefit if you can play the games on a track (or the perimeter of a field) that is at least a tenth of a mile in length. In inclement weather, edit the lesson and complete it in your home or, better still, go to a local indoor facility.

Don't forget to take holidays and vacations into account. Too much time between lessons will interfere with the continuity of the process. I recommend a September through November or a March through May schedule. Don't forget to consider severe weather conditions and changes in the number of daylight hours as winter's cold approaches.

Each activity follows a specific structure: an Introduction; a Getting on Board, which brings the focus onto the activity; Processing, which facilitates open discussion of the activity's goals; a Warm-Up, which prepares both body and mind for the physical activity to follow; the Workout, a fun active game that explores the day's lesson; and Final Processing, which helps provide closure. The amount of time allotted each lesson is about one to one and a quarter hours. Don't worry if you take longer than an hour to complete the lesson. But do be sure to allot at least an hour of uninterrupted time for you and your girl(s) to share the experience.

Most lessons require a few important supplies. Right now, take some time to put the following items in a workout bag:

16 8½-by-11-inch manila envelopes

A set of markers

6 ballpoint pens

1 roll of Scotch tape

2 pairs of scissors

A kitchen timer

A thick rope, about 6 feet long

A stack of blank paper

2 cameras with at least 20 exposures each (throwaway cameras are fine)

4 small orange cones or beanbags (these will indicate turnaround points for some of the games)

2 spiral notebooks or journals

MAKING THE LESSONS STICK

There are a number of ways that you can insure that the lessons will "stick" for you and your girl.

1. The adult should read through the lesson at least once before beginning. While the lessons are written in a very simple, easily understandable format, it is considerably more effective when the adult knows what is going to happen before the lesson starts.

2. Take a few minutes at the end of each lesson to summarize the events of the hour by each of you writing down some comments in your journals. Even better, later that day, you might each take time to write down your feelings about what you learned and the value of the lesson for you.

3. Take a photo at the end of each lesson, preferably with both of you in it. Somehow indicate the lesson number in the photo. At the conclusion of the ten weeks, line the photos up in chronological order. You will, unquestionably, notice changes in body language, both with each other and in how you hold yourselves. Take note of the increase in confident posture or fitness levels. Memorialize the experience in some way by putting the photos in a photo album or arranging them in a calendar or time line on a wall or shelf in your home.

4. Conclude the ten-week experience with the two of you participating in a 5K run/walk either in your hometown or a night's drive away. Determine what that event will be right now—at the beginning. Go ahead and register for it. You can get a list of local running events from a running store in your area. For regional events, check out *Runner's World* magazine. By registering now, you can keep your goal in sight and will be more likely to follow through. Don't worry about your fitness level right now. You *will* be ready to participate in a 5K by the end of the ten-week experience.

5. In Girls on the Run we give energy awards instead of trophies, toys, or trinkets. An energy award can be as

simple as a hug accompanied by the words "Way to go. You did *great* today!" Or it can be more elaborate, such as some kind of fun dance that the two of you make up for a job done well. You can get as silly as you want with these. Give an energy award to each other when someone does something that may have pushed them a little bit. Give yourself an energy award. Avoid promising food, toys, or trips for good efforts.

(An example of a silly energy award, and one of my favorites, that we give in Girls on the Run is the WOW. To give a WOW, open your mouth into a wide O shape and then hold up the number three using your three middle fingers on each hand on either side of the O. Look in the mirror. You have just formed the word *wow* with your hands and your mouth. If you are doing this with your daughter, she can get a little sillier and give you a WOW MOM by turning her fingers upside down to form the letter *M* on either side of her mouth. The idea is to get as silly as you possibly can. Silly is good—it gets us out of our adult skin and reminds us just how fun life can be!)

6. Most critical to the experience's being a positive and bonding one is keeping the games fun and energetic. Yes, there will be days when one or both of you are tired. I can promise you that if you go ahead and complete the lesson you will be energized by the end of the hour. Your relationship will go through a number of stages as you cover the ten-week terrain. At some point you may enter a storming phase— where boundaries are challenged and attitudes may turn a little negative. Don't give up. Storming is a good

thing. The lesson it teaches is invaluable. You *will* get through it and learn that, in life, there are times when we may not agree—or even get along, for that matter. But we can push through it with the people that we love and come out stronger on the other side!

A FEW IMPORTANT TIPS ON RUNNING OR WALKING

First, if you have *any* kind of physical health issue, check with your doctor. If either of you experience high blood pressure, asthma, high cholesterol, or any orthopedic problems, walking may be the better choice. Again, check with your doctor for his/her recommendation on how best to proceed.

Running is not for everyone. If you do not like to run and find walking more fulfilling, do it. Bigger people may not enjoy running as much as someone with a smaller build. The effort required by a big person to cover three miles is larger than for a smaller person, and the impact to joints and bones is more substantial. Do what you enjoy and encourage your girl to do the same. If you can afford it, get a good pair of running shoes. Taking the time to go to a specialty running store is worth it. A knowledgeable sales clerk can outfit you in a shoe that corresponds to the way your foot strikes the ground whether you are running or walking.

Between the warm-up and the workout you should allot time for stretching. You will see a list of recommended stretches at the conclusion of this chapter. The most effective stretching occurs after you have warmed up your body a little bit. A warm-up increases blood flow to your muscles and joints and insures safer stretching—as opposed to stretching completely cold.

Kids will always start a run by going all out and then losing steam after the first three to five minutes. Their little bodies have gone into what is called "oxygen debt," which is not usually a pleasurable experience. I encourage you both to pace yourselves. It is far better to start off slow and increase your speed as the workout progresses.

Everyone has his or her own running style. I personally have a relatively long stride for my five-foot-five frame. You need to find the stride that works best for you. Don't try to match each other's strides step for step. Carry your arms in a relaxed manner with your elbows at about a 90-degree or larger angle. Make sure your shoulders are relaxed and not bunched up around your ears. Your foot should strike the ground heel-first, followed by midfoot and then toe. Elite runners tend to land more on the midfoot and sprinters generally plant farther up on their toes. Unless you fall into the elite category, consider a heel-strike stride.

Whenever you get tired, one of the first places you should check for tension is your face. Is your mouth relaxed? Is your tongue loose in your mouth, or are you pressing it tightly to the top of your mouth? Are your eyebrows furrowed or relaxed? Are your neck and shoulders loose? The more relaxed the unused muscles of your body are, the more energy you have to expend toward the working muscles in your legs, midsection, and arms while you run.

And when in doubt—if you just don't think you can go any further—smile. I recently read about a study where a person's energy actually increases when they smile. So even if you have to fake a smile, do it. Your body will follow suit and your energy will increase.

So are you ready? Okay, hold onto your socks and prepare for a fun, fulfilling exploration of self, relationships, and love! The goals of the ten-week program are for the two of you to come out on the other side with an increase in self-love, self-acceptance, and a strong belief in yourselves and the limitless possibilities that stretch out before you.

THE JOURNEY

Ten Weeks of Activities for Growing and Learning Together

WEEK ONE:

Lesson One: Getting to Know Each Other
Lesson Two: Making Promises to Each Other

WEEK TWO:

Lesson Three: Taking My Own Inventory:
Assessing My Current Set of Needs, Wants, and Habits
Lesson Four: Let's Get Physical:
Being Physically Healthy

WEEK THREE:

Lesson Five: It's Okay to Be Emotional:
Being Emotionally Healthy
Lesson Six: It's Cool to Be Myself

WEEK FOUR:

Lesson Seven: Finding the Spirit in Me:
Being Spiritually Healthy
Lesson Eight: Life's Balance Beam:
Maintaining Balance in a Crazy World

WEEK FIVE:

Lesson Nine: Life Is the Ultimate Rush:
Steering Clear of Tobacco, Alcohol, and Other Drugs
Lesson Ten: Beauty Is an Inside Job:
Avoiding Eating Disorders

WEEK SIX:

Lesson Eleven: I Believe . . .

What Do I Believe, Anyway?

Lesson Twelve: Hello—Are You in There?

All About Good Listening Skills

WEEK SEVEN:

Lesson Thirteen: The Importance of Cooperation

Lesson Fourteen: Body Talk:

The Messages We Give with Our Bodies, Our Voices, and Our Actions

WEEK EIGHT:

Lesson Fifteen: Gossip Hurts:

How to Stop a Gossip Chain

Lesson Sixteen: Be Positive Is Not a Blood Type:

The Importance of Having a Positive Attitude

WEEK NINE:

Lesson Seventeen: Purple People Eater:

The Importance of *Not* People Pleasing and How to Stand Up for Yourself

Lesson Eighteen: Letting Go to Grow:

Letting Go of the People, Places, and Things Over Which We Have No Control

WEEK TEN:

Lesson Nineteen: Making Amends:

Learning to Say You're Sorry

Lesson Twenty: Sharing Our Love for Each Other

ONE: GETTING TO KNOW EACH OTHER

Objective

1. To provide us with the opportunity to learn more about each other
2. To introduce the concepts of the ten-week program
3. To introduce the various components of each lesson

Materials

❏ Interview questions to be asked by Adult (see page 123)
❏ Interview questions to be asked by Girl (see page 122)
❏ Two manila envelopes
❏ Scissors
❏ Markers
❏ Rope for designating a starting point
❏ Cones or beanbags for turnaround point

Introduction

Either Girl or Adult reads the following out loud:

"Today we will be learning new things—and maybe not so new things—about each other. We will also learn all about how the lessons we will do together over the next ten weeks will work. But first, Mom [or Adult] needs to read the following out loud:

"This activity is called a visualization. A visualization is where you envision something in your imagination—it's almost like you are actually experiencing it just as you are thinking about it. Okay, we are going to do a visualization together.

"First of all, picture bright white light that rests just on the inside of your body—maybe right where your heart is. That light is so bright, and when we are feeling good about ourselves it just shines out of us—through our eyes, our fingertips, in the way we walk, and stand up tall and straight. That white light is the very essence of who we are. It is what makes us special, unique, and beautiful on the inside.

"Now picture a large socket in the top of your head—kind of like a socket that is in the wall where you plug in an electrical appliance. Okay, got it? Can you see it in the top of your head? Okay, now imagine a huge cord going into that socket. But this cord is really yucky—it's got gooey, sticky, slow-moving, mucky liquid flowing through it. And also coming in through this cord are some messages we might get sometimes, messages like, 'you're not thin enough,' 'you're not pretty enough,' 'you're not sporty enough,' 'you don't have cool clothes,' 'you aren't very smart,' or maybe 'you shouldn't ever get angry' and even, 'it's not okay to cry.' When this brown stuff and these messages go into our brains and kind of ooze down into our body, we feel yucky—the brown stuff begins to put out that bright light, like syrup oozing down on your pancakes in the morning—we don't stand up as tall, we might feel sad a lot, or we might skip doing some exciting activities we'd like to try. We just don't feel good about ourselves with this brown cord coming into our spirits.

"Okay now, here's the fun part. We each need to take our right hand and gently pull that cord right out of our head. Okay, pull it out and throw it right behind you, somewhere far away. So now that that cord isn't in there anymore the light can shine again. It might even be multicolored, like a rainbow. It glitters, sparkles, and shines right out of the socket in the top of our head—out through our eyes and fingertips. We stand up tall and believe in ourselves. We express everything we are feeling. We know that we are wonderful. We know that we are perfect just the way we are! This is what this book is all about. Helping the two of us realize how special we are, each of us as individuals but also as a wonderful team together!!!

"So we need to promise each other that anytime we are

having a brown, muck-filled-cord kind of day, we will ask each other to help unplug us from those negative messages and feelings and let the colorful, sparkly, positive light in each of us shine. Can we promise this to each other?"

Getting on Board

❑ Using the interview sheets on pages 122 and 123, ask each other one question at a time. Girl should ask Adult one of her questions and record the answer, and then Adult will ask one of *her* questions and record the answer. Alternate until all the questions are answered.

Processing

Each of you should ask the other:

▶ How did it feel to ask each other these questions?
▶ How did it feel to answer them?
▶ What was the easiest question for you to answer? Why do you think it was easy to answer?
▶ Was there a question that you really had to think hard about before you could answer? Why do you think it was hard to answer?
▶ Was there a question that you were a little nervous about answering? Which one and why?

Warm-Up Activity

❑ Use the scissors to cut out each individual interview question. Adult, you need to cut out the questions you asked Girl into long strips and stack them on top of one another.
❑ Girl, you need to cut out the questions you asked Adult into long strips and stack them on top of one another. Don't mix yours up with Adult's.

❏ Take the two envelopes and label one SURPRISED and the other NOT SURPRISED and place them about fifty yards away from a designated starting point. You might designate the starting point by a small rope placed horizontally at your feet.

❏ Determine who will go first in this relay.

❏ On the count of three, the first person will run/walk/skip to the labeled envelopes and place one of her question strips into the appropriate envelope. For example, if she was surprised by the answer given for question one, she would place that in the surprised envelope. She puts only *one* question strip into an envelope on this run.

❏ She then returns to tag her partner who then takes off running/walking/skipping to place one of *her* question strips in the appropriate envelope.

❏ Continue until all ten questions have been placed in one of the labeled envelopes. (Each person will run a total of ten times to and from the envelopes.)

❏ When you are done, do some kind of energy award for each other. You can make one up or do a WOW.

Processing

▶ Open the envelopes.

▶ Go through the Surprised envelope together.

▶ Explain to each other why you were surprised and what you had expected instead of the answer you got.

▶ Did you learn anything new about each other? What?

▶ Were you surprised that you learned something new?

▶ What are some areas of the other person's life that you would like to know more about?

Stretch

❑ For a list of stretches see the end of this chapter.

Workout

❑ Determine the lap distance you will cover. (Are you at a track, or do you need to mark some "lap" space around your yard/parking lot/park with small cones or some other item?)

❑ Take a paper and write SOMETHING I HAVE WANTED TO ASK BUT NEVER HAVE across the top.

❑ Place this at your starting rope along with two markers.

❑ When you are each ready, begin running/walking/ skipping/moving forward around the designated lap. You may decide you want to move together or separately (or some combination of both). Each time you complete a lap, use a marker to write down one question you would like to ask the other person but never have.

❑ Continue until you have about fifteen minutes remaining in your session.

Final Processing

▶ Take a few minutes to read some of the questions to each other and if you want to answer them, go ahead. If you do not want to answer a question, that is certainly your right.

▶ Did you learn more new things about each other? Like what?

▶ How does it feel to know that you don't know everything there is to know about each other?

▶ How do you feel right now, after having moved your bodies for an hour?

▶ Tell each other what you like most about having one-on-one time together.

▶ Take a few minutes to write down in your own journal what you learned today.

▶ Snap a photo of each other holding up your workout question sheet.

▶ Thought for the day: "Even a one-thousand-mile journey needs a first step."

▶ Give each other a hug and a high-five.

QUESTIONS FOR GIRL TO ASK

(Photocopy for easy use.)

1.) How old were you when you kissed a boy for the first time?

2.) What accomplishment are you most proud of?

3.) What kind of vacation would you like to take?

4.) What is the first thing you do when you are really, really, really mad?

5.) Where did you go on your honeymoon (if you went on one)?

6.) What is the hardest physical challenge you've ever encountered?

7.) What do you like about growing older?

8.) What part of your body do you like the most?

9.) What color hair did you have when you were my age?

10.) Of all the houses you've ever lived in, which one did you like the most and why?

QUESTIONS FOR ADULT TO ASK

(Photocopy for easy use.)

1.) What is the best vacation you've ever been on?

2.) When was the last time you were embarrassed? What happened?

3.) Who is your favorite music group?

4.) What was the time you laughed the hardest?

5.) What do you do when you are really, really mad?

6.) What kind of clothes or outfit would make you feel really uncomfortable if you wore them?

7.) Who is your very best friend and why?

8.) If you and I had a weekend to do whatever we could, what would you like to do?

9.) What sport or recreational activity would you like to learn?

10.) What do you want to be when you grow up and why?

TWO: MAKING PROMISES TO EACH OTHER

Objective

1. To provide us with the opportunity to learn more about each other
2. To make promises to each other about what we will give of ourselves during the ten-week program
3. To make promises to each other about what we will give to our relationship generally

Materials

❏ Scotch tape
❏ Two manila envelopes
❏ Scissors
❏ Markers
❏ Rope for designating a starting point

Introduction

Either Girl or Adult reads the following out loud:

"Today we are going to be talking about promises. Promises are very important to keeping a relationship honest, forthright, and REAL. Promises are like pacts. When I promise I'm going to do something, one of the best gifts I can give my friend is keeping that promise. Sometimes, for whatever reason, keeping a promise isn't possible. Things come up, and when they do I need to let my friend know that I won't be able to keep the promise."

Getting on Board

❏ Together make a list of promises you want to make to each other to hold tight the bonds of your friendship/relationship. You need to come up with at least twenty promises.

Processing

Each of you should ask the other:

▶ Are any of these promises ones that only one of us needs to keep? Which promises do we need to keep?
▶ Can you group your promises into categories, like house chores, emotional health, school, or work promises? What other categories?
▶ Was there a promise that you haven't kept that you need to work on?

Warm-Up Activity

❏ Using the scissors, cut the list of promises into strips, with each promise on a separate strip.
❏ Place the strips into a pile at the starting point of what will be a fun relay.
❏ You can mark the starting point of your relay with a rope.
❏ Now label one manila envelope with the words *I am good at keeping this promise.*
❏ Label another manila envelope with the words *I need to work on keeping this promise better.*
❏ Place the envelopes about twenty-five yards away from the rope starting line.
❏ On the count of three, each of you needs to take a promise and run it as quickly as possible (remember you *are* warming up, though) to the envelope that is most appropriate for that promise. (For example, if you are good at keeping the promise you picked, put it in the *I Am Good at Keeping This Promise* envelope; if you need to work on the promise you picked, put it in the *I Need to Work on Keeping This Promise* envelope.)
❏ Run back and grab another promise and continue the warm-up until all slips are in an envelope.

❏ Note: Both of you are warming up at the same time.

❏ When you are done, do some kind of energy award for each other. You can make one up or do a WOW.

Processing

▸ Open the envelopes.

▸ Go through the envelopes together.

▸ Do you agree with each other on the promises in the Need Work envelope? How about the other envelope?

▸ Ask each other, "Do you feel like there is a promise you would like to add to the list?"

▸ Ask each other, "How good are you at following through on promises?"

▸ What did you learn about yourselves by doing this Warm-Up together?

Stretch

❏ For a list of stretches see the end of this chapter.

Workout

❏ Lay down the rope as a starting point, somewhere on the track you are using or at a point in the field or yard where you are running laps.

❏ Write the phrase *Promises we make to each other* on a piece of paper and place it next to the starting-line rope.

❏ Place the roll of Scotch tape next to it.

❏ On the count of three, take one of the promise slips from either envelope and run a lap with it.

❏ Think about that promise while you run. Consider the last time you followed through on that promise. Do you need to follow through on this promise more often?

❏ When you are done with the lap, tape the promise strip

to the page that is labeled PROMISES WE MAKE TO EACH
OTHER.

❑ Between the two of you, try to run at least sixteen laps.
❑ You may choose to run side by side or separately and at
your own pace. It's up to you two, but be sure to discuss
with each other before you start.
❑ Continue until you have about fifteen minutes
remaining in your session.

Final Processing

▶ Was one of your promises "To always try my best"? Did
you follow through on that promise *today*?
▶ You will need to post these promises in a prominent
place that the two of you see fairly often.
▶ Each of you pick out four different promises from the
sheet. Alternate reading them out loud to each other.
Make sure when you read the promise out loud you add
the phrase *I promise to* _____. For example, "I
promise to do my homework every day."
▶ Why do you think it is important to say these promises
out loud to each other?
▶ How do you feel right now, after having moved your
bodies for an hour?
▶ Tell each other what you like most about having one-on-
one time together.
▶ Take a few minutes to write down in your own journal
what you learned today.
▶ Snap a photo of each other holding up your workout
promise sheet.
▶ Thought for the day: "Friendship is born from an
identity of spiritual goals—from common navigation
toward a star." (Antoine de Saint-Exupéry)
▶ Give each other a hug and a high five.

THREE: TAKING MY OWN INVENTORY

Assessing My Current Set of Needs, Wants, and Habits

Objective

1. To assess where I am with certain behaviors and consider changing negative ones
2. To understand the concept of "taking inventory"
3. To increase our understanding of our own weaknesses and consider ways to turn them into strengths

Materials

❏ Two big boxes
❏ Paper
❏ Markers
❏ Scissors
❏ Scotch tape
❏ Rope for designating starting point
❏ Cones or beanbags to indicate workout area, if necessary

Introduction

Either Girl or Adult reads the following out loud:

"Today we will be learning about taking our own inventory. When a clerk in a store takes inventory of things on the shelves, he is going down the aisles and seeing how many of each item the store has. 'Let's see,' he might say as he studies his shelves with a clipboard, pen, and paper. 'We have twenty boxes of paper towels, six boxes of paper plates, and two boxes of plastic forks.' Now he knows he needs to put more boxes of plastic forks on the shelf but doesn't need to worry about the paper towels—not yet, anyway. Taking our own inventory is a little like that. Every once in a while it is important to pause to consider behaviors that are on our 'personality shelf' that we either need to replenish, remind ourselves to do more often, or consider removing from the shelf altogether. Today we will be considering some of those negative behaviors and ways we might remove them from our daily living."

Getting on Board

❏ Adult says to Girl, "Okay—help me with this math problem. Do I say '9 + 6 *is* 14' or '9 + 6 *are* 14'?"

❏ Girl will more than likely repeat "9 + 6 *is* 14."

❏ This exercise is about focus. Note the correct answer is 9 + 6 is *15* (not 14).

❏ Here is another one. Adult says to Girl: "Spell folk." Give Girl a chance to spell *folk*. Then ask her to spell *choke*. Give her a chance to spell *choke*. Now ask her, "What do you call the white part of the egg?" She will more than likely answer, "The yolk."

Processing

Each of you should ask the other:

▶ What did you learn about focus?

▶ Do we sometimes do activities that are habits that we aren't even aware of?

▶ Can you think of an activity or behavior that you do that you may not be aware of until someone points it out? (Do you bite your nails, talk negatively about other people, or have a facial twitch?)

Warm-Up Activity

❏ You will need two big boxes for this activity. (If you don't have two big boxes, two towels will work.)

❏ Label one of the boxes BEFORE and the other one AFTER.

❏ Label a piece of paper with the word BEFORE.

❏ Label another piece of paper with the word AFTER.

❏ Together, on the page labeled BEFORE, list at least six

habits or behaviors each of you do that you'd like to consider stopping or cutting back on. You may need to help each other determine what they are. You will have a total of twelve habits/behaviors written down.

❑ Now, on another piece of paper, write down a positive behavior that could go along with the negative one you would like to change. For example, you might counter "I bite my nails" on the Before page with "I take care of my hands" on the After page, or before: "I am always late"; after: "I am usually on time." Make sure to phrase the after behavior in a positive way. Take care not to use words like *not*, *no*, or *don't* in the phrase.

❑ With a pair of scissors, cut up the Before and After phrases, making sure to keep them separate.

❑ Put all the After phrases in the After box and hold on to your Before behaviors.

❑ Place the boxes twenty-five yards apart, like this:

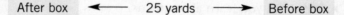

After box ◄——— 25 yards ———► Before box

Starting line

❑ On the count of three, Adult should take one of the Before behaviors, run to the Before box and throw it in there, and then run to the After box and pick up an After behavior. She should then run back to Girl, who then takes one of the Before behaviors, runs it to the Before box, and then picks up an After behavior.

❑ Do this until all the Before behaviors are in the Before box and all the After behaviors are in your hands.

❑ When you are done, do some kind of energy award for each other. You can make one up or do a WOW.

Processing

▶ Why do you think it was important to throw away the Before behaviors and pick up the After behaviors?

▶ Why do we need to know what our negative or unhealthy behaviors are? Open the envelopes.

▶ Can you think of any unhealthy behaviors you would like to change?

▶ Why was it important to name the After behaviors using all positive language?

Stretch

❑ For a list of stretches see the end of this chapter.

Workout

❑ Determine the lap distance you will cover. (Are you at a track, or do you need to mark some "lap" space around your yard/parking lot/park with small cones or some other item?) Use the rope to label the starting point.

❑ Label a blank piece of paper with Adult's name and the other with Girl's name.

❑ Attach those to your starting point with the roll of Scotch tape.

❑ Today you will run/walk together. As you complete each lap, tape the After behavior that you are holding onto the piece of paper with the person's name who would like to possess this After attitude or behavior.

❑ Be sure to do the laps together today. If you like, discuss the After behaviors as you walk/run.

❑ If you are new to running, try walking one lap and then jogging—very slowly—another lap.

❏ You are done when all of the After behaviors have been taped to the appropriately labeled pieces of paper.

Final Processing

▶ How do you feel right now, after having moved your bodies for an hour?

▶ Each of you should read the six positive behaviors on your sheet to the other person.

▶ Why do you think it is important to say these out loud to each other?

▶ What can you do the next time you find yourself using one of your negative Before habits/behaviors?

▶ What if you notice the other person doing one of her negative habits or behaviors?

▶ Is there a gentle way to point this out to her?

▶ Determine a place where you are going to post your positive After behaviors sheet.

▶ Tell each other what you like most about having one-on-one time together.

▶ Take a few minutes to write down in your own journal what you learned today.

▶ Snap a photo of each other holding up your workout question sheet.

▶ Thought for the day: "The people in our lives are often teachers of what we need to learn about ourselves."

▶ Give each other a hug and a high-five.

FOUR: LET'S GET PHYSICAL

Being Physically Healthy

Objective

1. To understand what it means to be physically healthy
2. To assess current healthy habits
3. To examine closely our eating habits and the ways we take care of ourselves physically

Materials

- ❏ Paper
- ❏ Bingo cards (see pages 139 and 140)
- ❏ Healthy Habit cards (see page 138)
- ❏ Rope for designating a starting point
- ❏ Scotch tape
- ❏ Markers

Introduction

Either Girl or Adult reads the following out loud:

"Today we are talking about what it means to be physically healthy. Let's take a minute and think about someone we know who is physically healthy. Can we think of anyone? What makes them healthy? Being physically healthy doesn't just mean eating right. It also means getting plenty of exercise, sleep, rest, and fun in our physical habits."

Getting on Board

- ❏ Label three pieces of paper: one with the word *food*; one with the word *exercise*; and one with the word *hygiene*.
- ❏ Arrange those pieces of paper in the following manner with about 5 yards between each.

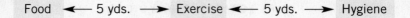

Food ◄——— 5 yds. ———► Exercise ◄——— 5 yds. ———► Hygiene

You are here behind the rope.

❑ On the count of three, Girl runs to the Hygiene sheet and yells out a healthy habit that she does regarding her physical hygiene (for example, "I brush my teeth at least twice a day").
❑ She waits there for Adult, who runs to her and yells out a healthy hygiene habit of her own.
❑ Then Girl runs to the next page, Exercise, and yells out a healthy habit she exhibits regarding exercise (for example, "I love to skate").
❑ Then Adult joins her there and yells out an exercise habit she does.
❑ Girl then runs to the final page, Food and yells out a healthy eating habit, and Adult joins her and does the same.
❑ Continue through the Healthy Habit "chain" four times.

Processing

Each of you should ask the other:

▸ Were there any healthy habits your partner stated that *you* need to work on?
▸ Were there any other habits you didn't get a chance to say out loud?
▸ What is a healthy habit you really need to work on to improve your physical health?

Warm-Up Activity

❑ Find the Healthy Habit cards at the end of this lesson.

❑ Cut them out and divide them between the two
   of you.
❑ Now leave the pieces of paper with the words *food*,
   exercise, and *hygiene* where they are.
❑ This time mark a starting point as indicated below.

| Food | ← | Exercise | → | Hygiene |

_____
Starting line

❑ On the count of three, Girl runs to one of the pieces of
   paper and throws an appropriate Healthy Habit card on
   top of it. For example, if she is holding the card that
   says WASHES HANDS BEFORE EACH MEAL she should put that
   on the Hygiene sheet. (If it is a really windy day,
   consider putting the beanbags down on the papers to
   keep them from blowing away.)
❑ Girl runs back to Adult and tags her, and then Adult
   goes and puts one of her Healthy Habit cards on the
   appropriate piece of paper.
❑ Each person will run a total of ten times, until all of
   their Healthy Habit cards are gone.
❑ When you are done, do some kind of energy award for
   each other. You can make one up or do a WOW.

Processing

▶ Retrieve the pieces of paper, making sure to keep the
   Healthy Habit cards with the appropriate category.
▶ Did you each get your Healthy Habit cards on the right
   category?

▸ Were there any Healthy Habit cards you would have added to the group?

▸ Are there any habits in particular that you need to work on doing more often?

Stretch

❑ For a list of stretches see the end of this chapter.

Workout

❑ Find the Healthy Habit Bingo cards on pages 139 and 140.

❑ Each of you should put your name on one of the bingo cards.

❑ Place your bingo cards at the starting point you have designated by the rope.

❑ Also, at the starting point, place all of the Healthy Habit cards in a small envelope.

❑ Every time you complete a lap take one of the Healthy Habit cards out of the envelope and paste it onto your bingo card.

❑ You can either run together or individually. Discuss this before you start the bingo game.

❑ When you have removed all the Healthy Habit cards from the envelope, the game is over.

Final Processing

▸ Did either one of you get bingo?

▸ If yes, give that person a high-five. If no, give yourselves a high-five anyway.

▸ Take a look at the bingo cards and discuss the healthy habits and ways that you can incorporate the ones you aren't doing into your life.

▸ Is there a place you can display these cards as a gentle reminder to yourselves?

▶ What is one healthy habit you promise to improve upon while you are doing these ten weeks together? Say it out loud to each other.

▶ Tell each other what you like most about having one-on-one time together.

▶ Take a few minutes to write down in your own journal what you learned today.

▶ Snap a photo of each other holding up your workout question sheet.

▶ Thought for the day: "A smile starts on the inside and works its way out."

▶ Give each other a hug and a high-five.

HEALTHY HABIT CARDS

(Photocopy for easy use.)

Brushes teeth at least twice per day	Washes hands before each meal
Eats at least three servings of protein every day	Eats at least five fruits and vegetables every day
Drinks plenty of lowfat milk	Enjoys desserts without feeling guilty about eating them
Gets plenty of sleep	Doesn't stay in sweaty workout clothes too long after a workout
Drinks plenty of water before, during, and after exercise	Makes sure to eat plenty of carbohydrates to fuel exercise
Exercises at least thirty minutes, three to four days per week	Exercises at least thirty minutes, three to four days per week
ALWAYS eats breakfast	Eats THREE well-balanced meals per day
Limits the amount of caffeine in her diet	Drinks juices more often than sodas
Takes a bath or shower at least every other day	Washes skin and hair well after swimming
Eats plenty of fiber	Gets plenty of calcium (cheese, milk, dairy) in her diet

HEALTHY HABIT BINGO CARDS

(Photocopy for easy use.)

Brushes teeth at least twice per day	Eats at least three servings of protein every day	Drinks plenty of lowfat milk
Gets plenty of sleep	Drinks plenty of water before, during, and after exercise	Washes hands before each meal
Eats at least five fruits and vegetables every day	Enjoys desserts without feeling guilty about eating them	Doesn't stay in sweaty workout clothes too long after a workout

HEALTHY HABIT BINGO CARDS

Exercises at least thirty minutes, three to four days per week	Always eats breakfast	Gets plenty of calcium (cheese, milk, dairy) in her diet
Eats plenty of fiber	Eats THREE well-balanced meals per day	Drinks juices more often than sodas
Limits the amount of caffeine in her diet	Enjoys desserts without feeling guilty about eating them	Takes a bath or shower at least every other day

FIVE: IT'S OKAY TO BE EMOTIONAL

Being Emotionally Healthy

Objective

1. To understand what it means to be emotionally healthy
2. To learn to identify our emotions and how they show themselves in our behavior and attitudes
3. To examine closely our emotional health and how we handle uncomfortable emotions

Materials

❏ Emotional Interview questions (see page 146)
❏ Two manila envelopes
❏ Scissors
❏ Markers
❏ Rope for designating a starting point

Introduction

Either Girl or Adult reads the following out loud:

"Today we are talking about what it means to be emotionally healthy. Let's take a minute and think about someone we know who is emotionally healthy. Can we think of anyone? What makes them emotionally healthy? Being emotionally healthy doesn't mean we are necessarily even-keeled. What it means is that we are able to express all of our emotions in a way that doesn't interfere with others' rights.

Getting on Board

❏ Think of an emotion.
❏ Act it out for the other person. Try to only use your facial expressions and body language. Don't use your voice.
❏ See if you can each act out at least three emotions.

Processing

Each of you should ask the other:

▶ Which emotion was easiest to guess? Why do you think that?

▶ Which one was the hardest to guess? Why?

▶ Which one of these emotions do you frequently feel?

▶ What is an emotion you sometimes try *not* to feel? Why? Do you think it is good for you to *not* feel it? Why or why not?

Warm-Up Activity

❑ Find the Emotion cards on page 145.

❑ Photocopy the cards and cut out and distribute them to each other, so that each of you has six.

❑ Label one manila envelope with the word *comfortable* and another one with the word *uncomfortable*.

❑ Mark a starting point for this relay with the rope and put the envelopes about twenty-five yards away, as indicated below.

Uncomfortable ◀———— 25 yards ————▶ Comfortable

———————
Starting line

❑ On the count of three, Girl takes one of her Emotion cards and runs it to the envelope that best describes the way she feels when she experiences that particular emotion. For example, if she picks the Anger card and she feels uncomfortable when she feels angry, she

should run her Emotion card to the Uncomfortable
envelope.
❑ She runs back to high-five Adult waiting for her at the
starting line.
❑ Now Adult runs with an Emotion card and puts it in the
appropriately labeled envelope.
❑ She returns and high-fives Girl.
❑ Continue this process until each person has run six
times.
❑ When you are done, do some kind of energy award for
each other. You can make one up or do a WOW.

Processing

▶ Pull out each emotion from the envelopes. See if you
both agree on whether that emotion makes you
comfortable or uncomfortable. (Just a note—When I was
young anger used to make me feel uncomfortable. Now
that I am older and have felt it more often over my life,
it doesn't make me uncomfortable anymore.)
▶ Why were the envelopes labeled COMFORTABLE and
UNCOMFORTABLE instead of GOOD and BAD?
▶ Why do you think we get more comfortable with all of
our emotions as we get older?
▶ Does everybody get angry sometimes?
▶ When was the last time you were really, really angry?
Share that with each other.

Stretch

❑ For a list of stretches see the end of this chapter.

Workout

❑ Find the Emotional Interview questions at the end of
this lesson.

❑ Place the sheet along with two markers/pens at the starting point of your laps.

❑ Mark your starting point with the rope.

❑ On the count of three, take off around the track. You may run together or separately today. Decide which way you would like to do the workout today.

❑ At the end of each lap answer one of the questions. Answer them in order and make sure that you each answer all of the questions.

❑ When each of you has answered all twelve of the questions, you are done.

Final Processing

▸ What is body language? How do we show our emotions using body language?

▸ How do our facial expressions reveal our emotions?

▸ Why is it important to express all of our emotions?

▸ What happens if we only show some of our emotions?

▸ What emotion are you feeling right now?

▸ Adult, express how you feel toward Girl.

▸ Girl, express how you feel toward Adult.

▸ Take a few minutes to write down in your own journal what you learned today.

▸ Snap a photo of each other holding up your workout question sheet.

▸ Thought for the day: "I would not exchange the laughter of my heart for the fortunes of the multitudes; nor would I be content with converting my tears . . . into calm. It is my fervent hope that my whole life on this earth will ever be tears and laughter." (Kahlil Gibran)

▸ Give each other a hug and a high-five.

EMOTION CARDS
(Photocopy for easy use.)

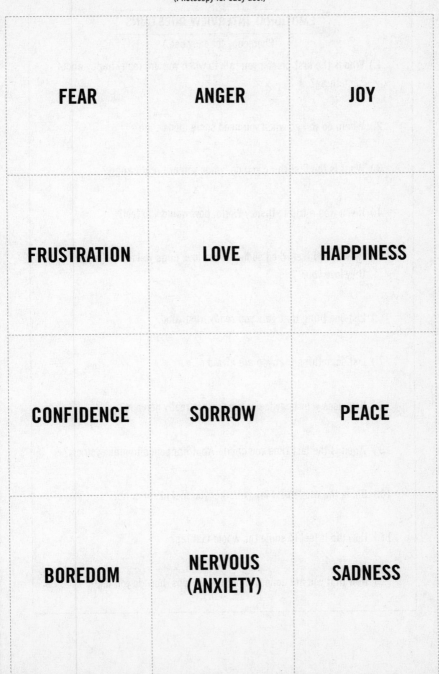

FEAR	ANGER	JOY
FRUSTRATION	LOVE	HAPPINESS
CONFIDENCE	SORROW	PEACE
BOREDOM	NERVOUS (ANXIETY)	SADNESS

EMOTIONAL INTERVIEW QUESTIONS

(Photocopy for easy use.)

1.) Who is the first person you talk to when you are really happy about something?

2.) Where do you go when you need some alone time?

3.) What is the first thing you do, when you are *really* angry?

4.) If you won a trip to Disney World, how would you feel?

5.) How do you feel when someone you love hugs you and tells you they love you?

6.) List one thing that gets you *really* frustrated.

7.) List something that you are afraid of.

8.) How does your body feel when you are really nervous?

9.) When is the last time you cried? What happened to make you cry?

10.) Smile the whole next lap, whether you feel like it or not.

11.) How did it feel to smile the whole last lap?

12.) Now that you are done with all twelve laps, how do you feel?

SIX: IT'S COOL TO BE MYSELF

Objective

1. To understand the importance of celebrating our strengths
2. To explore attitudes around letting our real selves show
3. To examine closely our own stereotyping around the ways girls "should" act instead of what really lets our true spirits shine

Materials

❑ Paper
❑ Markers
❑ Scissors
❑ Rope for designating a starting point
❑ Cone or beanbag to designate turnaround point

Introduction

Either Girl or Adult reads the following out loud:

"Today we are talking about how cool it is to be ourselves. Sometimes girls don't act as smart as they are. Or sometimes they don't let themselves excel in sports because they worry others might think they are too much like a tomboy. Why do you think they don't act smart? Think about some television shows and the girls on the show. Are the girls on those shows sometimes one-dimensional? In other words, do the girls on some shows show only a part of themselves? Today we are going to explore what it means to *totally* be ourselves."

Getting on Board

❑ Each of you should take a minute and draw a picture of a butterfly on a piece of paper.

❑ Use the markers to decorate the wings and make your butterfly as beautiful as possible.

❑ Show your butterfly to each other.

❑ Make any comments you would like about your butterfly or the other person's butterfly.

Processing

Each of you should ask the other:

▶ How did you feel drawing this picture of a butterfly?

▶ How do you feel when you take time to really watch a beautiful butterfly on a bright and sunny day?

▶ What would our world be like if all of the beautiful butterflies in the world just went away and hid in the bushes where we couldn't see them?

▶ Do we all have traits—both on the outside and on the inside—that are beautiful?

Warm-Up Activity

❑ Without letting each other see, both Adult and Girl make a list of traits that each thinks are remarkable about the other. For example if Girl thinks that Adult is a *great cook*, she should write that down. Perhaps she "is good at making *me* feel good about myself." Each person should write down ten strengths of character that they believe make the other person beautiful. Adult might write, *she is really, really smart.* Girl may need some assistance with this activity.

❑ Cut your lists into "strength strips" and keep them hidden from the other person.

❑ You will need to mark a starting point with the rope and place a cone (or beanbag) about thirty yards away.

❑ Now Girl hands Adult one of her strengths (one that Girl wrote about Adult).

❑ Adult reads it out loud *loudly* and takes off running around the cone and back to the rope.

❑ Now Adult hands one of Girl's strengths to *her* (one that Adult wrote down about Girl). Girl reads it out loud *loudly* and takes off running around the cone.

❑ Take turns doing this until all of the strength strips have been handed to each other. Make sure to say them loudly before you take off running around the cone.

❑ When you are done, do some kind of energy award for each other. You can make one up or do a WOW.

Processing

▶ Were you surprised by any of the strengths the other person wrote down about you?

▶ Are there any strengths about yourself that you would add to the list?

▶ Why is it important to celebrate all of our strengths—all of our *selves*—with each other?

▶ Sometimes in ads and in TV shows, the most important thing about a girl is her looks. What do you think is most important about a girl?

Stretch

❑ For a list of stretches see the end of this chapter.

Workout

❑ Hold on to your strength slips.

❑ Today you will each run at your own pace and by yourself.

❑ Mark the start of your lap with the rope.

❑ Place your butterfly picture and a roll of Scotch tape by the starting-line rope.

❑ At the count of three, both of you start running.

❏ At the end of every lap, each of you tapes one of your strengths onto the butterfly you drew.

❏ You will each run a total of ten laps.

Final Processing

▶ At the beginning of the lesson we talked about the beauty of a butterfly. Why do you think your strengths are now taped on your butterfly?

▶ If you feel happy and joyous looking at the beauty of a butterfly, how do you think other people feel when they are with you when you are letting all of your beautiful strengths shine out?

▶ Who gets hurt when you don't let the beauty of your strengths shine out?

▶ Take a minute and tell the other person a strength in them that you really admire.

▶ Take a few minutes to write down in your own journal what you learned today.

▶ Snap a photo of each other holding up your workout butterfly sheet.

▶ Thought for the day: "The virtue of the candle lies not in the wax that leaves its trace, but in its light." (Antoine de Saint-Exupéry)

▶ Give each other a hug and a high-five.

SEVEN: FINDING THE SPIRIT IN ME

Being Spiritually Healthy

Objective

1. To understand what it means to be spiritually healthy
2. To identify ways to connect with the positive energy in and around us

3. To examine ways to slow down our quick-fix, overstimulating environment

Materials

❏ Rope for designating a starting point, if necessary

Introduction
Either Girl or Adult reads the following out loud:

"Today we are talking about what it means to be spiritually healthy. Being spiritually healthy is one of the most important keys to leading a balanced life. The only way to take care of our spiritual health is to take the time to work on it. This lesson will give us a chance to find a few moments with the Spirit inside of us."

Getting on Board

❏ Lie down on the grass next to each other.
❏ Stare up at the sky, the trees, the birds, the clouds, or the buildings, if you are totally urban. Listen to the sounds of nature or the city. Take in the scents around you.
❏ Lie still alongside each other.
❏ Don't talk at all.
❏ You may hold hands if you like.
❏ Move as little as possible.
❏ See how still you can be for ten minutes.
❏ Don't fall asleep.
❏ Set a timer for the ten minutes.
❏ At the end of the ten minutes, sit up.

Processing

Each of you should ask the other:

▶ What did you think about during the ten minutes?
▶ Were you comfortable or uncomfortable doing this activity? Why?

▸ Why is it important to take time out of each day to be still, quiet, and peaceful?

▸ Did you notice something that you wouldn't have normally noticed?

Warm-Up Activity

❏ Today there will be no warm-up.

Stretch

❏ For a list of stretches, see the end of this chapter.

Workout

❏ Today's workout is a tough one.

❏ The two of you will run/walk today as far as you can go in the remaining time.

❏ You may want to do today's workout at a park or nature trail (just be sure that you don't lose sight of each other).

❏ You may walk together or separately *but*: you may not talk to each other.

❏ You may hold hands or stroll arm in arm, *but absolutely no talking*.

❏ Continue until you have about ten minutes remaining in your session.

Final Processing

▸ How did you like today's workout?

▸ What did you think about?

▸ Did you learn anything new about yourself?

▸ Some people are social runners (they like to run with people). Others prefer to run alone and run quietly. What kind of runner are you? (You could be both.)

▶ What is meditation?

▶ Can you see how running or walking can be like meditation?

▶ Girl: Tell Adult one thing or person for whom you are thankful.

▶ Adult: Tell Girl one thing or person for whom you are thankful.

▶ Take a few minutes to write down in your own journal what you learned today.

▶ Snap a photo of each other holding up your workout question sheet.

▶ Thought for the day: "Be still and know that I am here."

▶ Give each other a hug and a high-five.

EIGHT: LIFE'S BALANCE BEAM

Maintaining Balance in a Crazy World

Objective

1. To introduce the concept of balance in our daily living
2. To explore the importance of balancing our lives
3. To explore the reasons women and girls may lead unbalanced lives

Materials

❑ Paper
❑ Markers
❑ Rope used for designating a starting point
❑ 1 spoon
❑ 1 penny or several raw eggs

Introduction

Either Girl or Adult reads the following out loud:

"Today we will be talking about leading a balanced life. What do we think balanced living is? Maintaining balance in our lives means taking enough time to replenish ourselves, while also giving time and attention to people and things in our life that are important to us."

Getting on Board

❏ Write each of the following words on a separate sheet of scratch paper: *family, school/work, self, friends.*

❏ Choose who will go first and place the four pieces of paper directly in front of her with about two inches between each page, like this:

Family ◄—2"—► School/Work ◄—2"—► Self ◄—2"—► Friends

You are standing right here.

❏ The first player now stands on her left foot first and gently lifts her right leg so that it is bent slightly behind her as she leans forward to touch each of the labeled pages with her right hand.

❏ She will be balancing on her left foot and gently touching each of the pages with her right hand. She cannot use her left hand to brace herself. Her left hand and arm are in a position to assist in her balancing on the left foot.

❏ Without putting her right foot down, player touches each of the papers four more times.

❏ Now the player repeats this process, but balances on her
right foot and touches each of the pages with her left
hand. Do this four more times.

❏ Allow the other person a chance to perform this
"balancing act."

Processing

Each of you should ask the other:

▸ Were you able to balance on one foot?

▸ Was one foot easier than the other?

▸ What happened if you began touching the papers
too fast?

▸ What happened if you began touching the papers
too hard?

▸ What did you learn about maintaining balance doing
this exercise?

Warm-Up Activity

❏ Now take each of the pages that were labeled FAMILY,
SCHOOL/WORK, SELF, and FRIENDS and put them at the four
corners of an imaginary square. Allow for about twenty
yards between each corner.

❏ Place the rope in a small circle in the middle of the
square. This will serve as your starting point.

❏ Now, on the count of three, Girl will start at the center,
run to one corner, and touch the paper with her hand.

❏ She will immediately run back to the center, touch the
rope with her hand, and then run to the next corner,
where she will touch it with her hand and then run back
to the center.

❏ She will continue this process until she has touched all
four corners and returned to the center.

❏ Adult will time her.

❏ Now give Girl a spoon and a coin (for lots of fun, instead of a coin, use a raw egg).

❏ Now on the count of three, Girl will repeat the same warm-up but now she has to keep the coin on the spoon at all times.

❏ Adult will time her. If Girl drops the coin, the clock doesn't stop—Girl simply has to start over while the clock keeps running.

❏ Now let Adult do the same warm-up.

❏ When you are done, do some kind of energy award for each other. You can make one up or do a WOW.

Processing

▶ How hard was this warm-up?

▶ Was it more difficult to do the activity quickly with the spoon and the coin?

▶ What does this say about the time needed to balance our lives?

▶ Does balancing our lives means slowing down and putting quality time toward those four areas of our lives as opposed to running at them recklessly?

▶ What were some of the major differences between the first time you ran to the corners and the second time you ran to the corners with the spoon and the coin?

▶ What does this game have to do with maintaining balance in our lives?

Stretch

❏ For a list of stretches see the end of this chapter.

Workout

❏ Today's workout is all about pacing.

❏ You will run or walk together.

❏ Mark off your lap if necessary.

❏ On the count of three, try to run the entire lap or run/walk it if necessary. Your goal is to try to run the entire way.

❏ Time yourselves. Do not run too fast. Make sure to pace yourselves.

❏ What was your time?

❏ Write that down on a piece of paper if you like.

❏ Now do another lap and try to get the exact same time for that lap. Use your watch to assist you if you like.

❏ Now do a third lap, but try to get as close to the same time *without looking at your watch*.

❏ Repeat for a total of two miles or until you have about ten minutes remaining in your session.

Final Processing

▸ How close were you to having the exact same time for each lap?

▸ Did you get closer with or without the watch?

▸ Sometimes maintaining balance in our lives means pacing ourselves. What do you think this means?

▸ What happens if you start out the laps way too fast?

▸ What happens if you just run around like crazy trying to get things done? Are you more or less efficient?

▸ Do you get more done when you actually pace yourself instead of spinning your wheels inefficiently?

▸ What did you learn about maintaining balance today?

▸ Tell each other what you like most about having one-on-one time together.

▸ Take a few minutes to write down in your own journal what you learned today.

▸ Snap a photo of each other holding up your workout question sheet.

▶ Thought for the day: "The best way to stay balanced is through self-respect. I slow down long enough to breathe deeply, count my blessings, and be peaceful in the moment."

▶ Give each other a hug and a high-five.

NINE: LIFE IS THE ULTIMATE RUSH

Steering Clear of Tobacco, Alcohol, and Other Drugs

Objective

1. To provide some factual information regarding tobacco, alcohol, and marijuana
2. To provide an open forum for Adult and Girl to discuss possible scenarios associated with drug use
3. To increase the lines of communication between Girl and Adult

Materials

❑ Drug Fact cards (see page 162)
❑ Drug Fact cards with answers (see page 163)
❑ Lap scenarios (see pages 164 to 165)
❑ Five manila envelopes
❑ Rope for designating starting point
❑ Markers
❑ Scissors

Introduction

Either Girl or Adult reads the following out loud:

"Last time we talked about maintaining balance. We've also talked about our physical, emotional, and spiritual health. Sometimes when a person's life gets completely out of whack, they turn to tobacco, alcohol, or other drugs to handle the stress. Or their life may become chaotic because of their tobacco, alcohol, or drug use. Today we are going to learn some facts about drugs and open the lines of communication between us so we can talk about this in the years to come."

Getting on Board

❑ Together make a list of five to ten reasons why you think a young girl smokes her first cigarette.

❑ When you have completed that, list ways that she can get the same result but through a healthier means. For example if you wrote, *She starts smoking to be more grown-up,* then a healthier alternative for her to be more grown-up might be *to volunteer at a local charity answering the telephone.*

Processing

Each of you should ask the other:

▸ How did it feel to talk about this issue with each other?

▸ Is there anyone in your immediate family who smokes? How do you feel about it?

▸ What did you learn about yourself doing this Getting on Board?

Warm-Up Activity

❑ Write one of the following words or phrases on each of your manila envelopes: *tobacco, alcohol, marijuana, marijuana and alcohol,* and *all three.*

❑ Place the envelopes in a circle around you with your starting-line rope in the center. Put them about twenty-five yards away from the center of the circle.

❑ Find the drug fact cards on page 162 and photocopy them and cut them out.

❑ Split them up so that you each have six cards.

❏ On the count of three, Girl should read her fact out loud and then, with the Adult, determine which drug pertains to that fact. She should then run the card to the appropriate envelope and put it in the envelope.

❏ She runs back to Adult, who reads out one of her facts and then, after they determine the appropriate drug, run it to the corresponding envelope.

❏ Continue until each person has run six times.

❏ When you are done, do some kind of energy award for each other. You can make one up or do a WOW.

Processing

▶ Open the envelopes.

▶ Go through the envelopes and the facts in them again.

▶ Check to see if you got them correct (the correct answers are on page 163).

▶ Why is it important to talk to each other about these kinds of issues?

▶ Is there a history of alcohol abuse in your family? Did you know that this increases your chances of carrying the gene for alcoholism? Discuss this with each other.

▶ What scares you most about the abuse of alcohol and other drugs?

Stretch

❏ For a list of stretches see the end of this chapter.

Workout

❏ Determine the lap distance that you will cover. Mark the starting line with the rope and place the lap scenario sheet (see pages 164 to 165) at the starting line.

❏ Starting with the scenario for Lap One, read it to each other and then discuss what you would do in each situation as you go around the lap. You may walk, run, skip—whatever you would like—but since you will be talking about the scenario, you will need to stay together.

❏ When you complete the first lap, read the second scenario and then discuss it on the next lap.

❏ Continue until you have covered approximately three miles. (Read as many of the twelve scenarios as you can.)

Final Processing

▶ What was it like to talk about these topics while you were running/walking?

▶ What did you learn about the other person?

▶ What did you learn about yourself?

▶ Would you be willing to sign a contract that states you will never smoke cigarettes?

▶ If so, do that right here.

▶ I promise to never start smoking cigarettes.

_____

(sign your name on this line)

▶ I promise to never start smoking cigarettes.

_____

(sign your name on this line)

▶ Take a few minutes to write down in your own journal what you learned today.

▶ Snap a photo of each other holding up your workout question sheet.

▶ Thought for the day: "The important thing is not to stop questioning." (Albert Einstein)

▶ Give each other a hug and a high-five.

Drug Fact Cards

(Photocopy for easy use.)

Use of this (or these) drug(s) increases a person's appetite.	Use of this (or these) drug(s) causes red eyes.
A person can get addicted to this (or these) drug(s).	It is illegal to possess this (or these) drug(s).
Use of this (or these) drug(s) impairs a person's ability to drive.	Use of this (or these) drug(s) increases the number of wrinkles on a person's face.
Use of this (or these) drug(s) may cause malnourishment.	Abuse of this (or these) drug(s) while a woman is pregnant may harm her developing baby.
Abuse of this (or these) drug(s) makes a person depressed.	Abuse of this (or these) drug(s) often leads a person into trouble financially and with the law.
Abuse of this (or these) drug(s) hurts not only the person taking the drug but those they love.	(Age appropriate) A girl who abuses this (or these) drug(s) is more likely to get pregnant as a teenager than one who doesn't.

Drug Fact Cards with Answers

(Photocopy for easy use.)

Use of this (or these) drug(s) increases a person's appetite.
MARIJUANA

Use of this (or these) drug(s) causes red eyes.
MARIJUANA

A person can get addicted to this (or these) drug(s).
ALL THREE

It is illegal to possess this (or these) drug(s).
MARIJUANA

Use of this (or these) drug(s) impairs a person's ability to drive.
ALCOHOL AND MARIJUANA

Use of this (or these) drug(s) increases the number of wrinkles on a person's face.
TOBACCO

Use of this (or these) drug(s) may cause malnourishment.
ALCOHOL

Abuse of this (or these) drug(s) while a woman is pregnant may harm her developing baby.
ALL THREE

Abuse of this (or these) drug(s) makes a person depressed.
ALCOHOL

Abuse of this (or these) drug(s) often leads a person into trouble financially and with the law.
ALCOHOL AND MARIJUANA

Abuse of this (or these) drug(s) hurts not only the person taking the drug but those they love.
ALL THREE

(Age appropriate) A girl who abuses this (or these) drug(s) is more likely to get pregnant as a teenager than one who doesn't.
ALL THREE

Lap Scenarios

Lap One: You get in the car with an adult who is driving and they have had too much to drink. During the next lap, discuss how you would handle the situation.

Lap Two: Your best friend takes up smoking cigarettes. What would you do about it?

Lap Three: Girl has been invited to a slumber party at a classmate's house. Rumors have it that the classmate's big brother smokes marijuana regularly. How would you two handle this situation?

Lap Four: Most girls that don't drink or smoke cigarettes before the age of twenty-one don't end up having a problem with it. Why do you think this is so?

(Age appropriate.) **Lap Five:** Girls who do not respect their bodies tend to get into unhealthy relationships.

Lap Six: Girl is at a friend's house and the friend pulls out a cigarette and starts smoking. What should Girl do?

Lap Seven: Sometimes people turn to cigarettes, alcohol, and other drugs to handle stress. Talk about stress and healthy ways to deal with it.

Lap Eight: The occurence of alcoholism is higher in families where there is a history of alcoholism in the family tree. Discuss the disease of alcoholism and any family members who suffer from it.

Lap Nine: Good communication between a young person and a caring adult is one of the best ways to keep that young person from smoking, drinking, or using drugs. What can you two do to always keep the lines of communication open between you?

Lap Ten: Sometimes girls start smoking because they want to be popular or think it's cool. Discuss other—healthy—ways you can be cool or popular without smoking.

Lap Eleven: Another way to prevent teenage smoking is by getting girls involved with a healthy group of friends—like sports teams, clubs, and other groups. Discuss possible clubs or groups that you would like to be a part of.

Lap Twelve: What would you like to say to each other about tobacco, alcohol, and other drugs?

TEN: BEAUTY IS AN INSIDE JOB

Avoiding Eating Disorders

Objective

1. To provide a healthy perception of beauty
2. To understand the role genetics plays in the shape of our bodies
3. To differentiate between standards of beauty as defined by our culture and beauty of character

Materials

❏ At least twenty pieces of blank paper or, better yet, index cards
❏ Two manila envelopes
❏ Markers

❏ Rope for designating a starting point
❏ Cones or beanbags to designate turnaround points
  for relay

Introduction
Either Girl or Adult reads the following out loud:
"When we look at all the fashion magazines, many of the
women have similar characteristics. They are mostly very thin
and young, and have certain features that are similar. Many
have long hair, and a lot of them don't wear much clothing.
Sometimes when we look at those magazines we begin to feel
like that is how *we* should look. But really, we have many
things about ourselves that make *us* beautiful. Beauty really has
nothing to do with how we look and much more to do with
how we act and feel. Today we will be taking a look at the difference between external beauty and the beauty of our character—
our spirit—the part of us that makes us special."

Getting on Board
❏ You will need an apple, a banana, and a pear for this
  activity. If you don't have those, draw them on a piece
  of paper.
❏ Put the banana on the table and give the pear to Girl
  and the apple to Adult.
❏ Try to make the pear and the apple look like the banana.
  This may require biting it, scratching it, cutting it—
  disfiguring it in some way to make it closer in shape to
  the banana.

Processing
Each of you should ask the other:
▶ Would you admit that many of the models in fashion
  magazines are shaped more like the banana?

- Describe the banana's shape.
- Now describe the shape of the apple and the pear.
- Describe their colors and textures and the way they taste.
- Would you admit that all three of these fruits are pretty and taste good?
- What kind of tree does an apple come from? What kind of tree does a pear come from? What about a banana?
- Would you ever see a pear growing on an apple tree or a banana growing on a pear tree?
- How are you and your parents like the apple, the pear, or the banana?
- What is genetics?
- Would a blond, blue-eyed white person ever be born to a black-haired, brown-eyed black person? (Not likely.)
- So do you see how, if our bodies are built a certain way, much of how we are put together has to do with the way our parents' bodies are put together?
- Are you big-boned, small-boned, or medium-boned?
- Are you of tall, short, or medium height?
- Are you of a thin, big, or medium build?
- Name the most beautiful thing about your body.

Warm-Up Activity

❏ First you each will need to list six things about yourself that make you physically beautiful. Maybe you have delicious red cheeks or scrumptious curly hair. Maybe you have a cool split between your two front teeth or freckles all across your face and body. Write these six things down on a piece of paper.
❏ On the back of the paper write down six things that describe the beauty of your character. For example, you

might be a very caring person. Or maybe you are very trustworthy. Perhaps you are loyal to your friends, or you take good care of your children.

❏ Place two cones about fifty yards apart. Start at one and, together, read aloud one of the traits that makes you beautiful on the outside.

❏ Then, together, run to the other cone and read out one of the things that describes the beauty of your character.

❏ Now run back to the first cone and read the second item on your list that describes your external beauty.

❏ Then run to the other cone and read the second item on your list that describes the beauty of your character.

❏ Continue until you've read all twelve items. Make sure to read them out loud and together.

Processing

▶ What is the difference between external beauty and beauty of character?

▶ What do we see when we see the models in the magazines?

▶ Can you think of a way you could photograph or draw a picture of someone that shows their strength of character?

▶ Why is it important to not judge people by their external beauty?

▶ Would you rather have an externally beautiful friend or someone with the wonderful beauty of strength, friendship, and character?

Stretch

❏ For a list of stretches see the end of this chapter.

Workout

❏ Determine the lap distance you will cover. Mark the starting line with the rope and place an envelope there labeled THE BEAUTY OF MY CHARACTER. You will also need to place some blank paper or index cards there, along with two markers.

❏ Every time you complete a lap, write down something that describes what makes you beautiful on the *inside*.

❏ Take the paper and place it in the envelope.

❏ Repeat this at the end of each lap.

❏ Continue running/walking laps until you have about five minutes remaining in your time together.

❏ You may run together or separately, or a combination of both.

Final Processing

▶ Open up the envelope and read the items in there to each other.

▶ What did you learn about the other person?

▶ What did you learn about yourself?

▶ The next time someone you know makes a negative comment about how someone looks or dresses, what can you do to emphasize the importance of their internal beauty?

▶ If the two of you live together, take this envelope home and place it in a place you will remember. Every morning pull out one of the Beauty cards/papers and place it in a position where you can see it. Let this be a constant reminder that *we are beautiful because of who we are, not how we look!!!!*

▶ If you don't live together, Adult takes half of the Beauty cards/papers and Girl takes the other half. Every day place one of these in a prominent place in your home to be a constant reminder that *we are beautiful not because of how we look, but because of who we are.*

▶ Take a few minutes to write down in your own journal what you learned today.

▶ Snap a photo of each other holding up your workout question sheet.

▶ Thought for the day: "Love is a seed; it has only to sprout, and its roots spread far and wide." (Antoine de Saint-Exupéry)

▶ Give each other a hug and a high-five.

ELEVEN: I BELIEVE . . .

What Do I Believe, Anyway?

Objective

1. To provide an opportunity to explore my values
2. To understand the role our values play in our behavior
3. To realize that others may have different values than us and to explore the importance of accepting these differences

Materials

❑ Paper
❑ Markers
❑ Rope for designating a starting point

Introduction
Either Girl or Adult reads the following out loud:
"What we value is at the core of everything we do. Do I make my bed first thing in the morning because I value self-discipline? Do

I return items I have borrowed from someone because I respect him/her? Am I on time because I respect others and their time? Today we will determine some of our values and what is important to us."

Getting on Board

❑ Read the following values out loud and come up with your own definition of them: Gratitude, Honesty, Self-Respect, Compassion, Acceptance. You might want to describe a situation where each value was important.

❑ Now think of some more values and list them on a piece of paper. Define them for yourselves.

Processing

Each of you should ask the other:

▶ What did you learn about yourself?

▶ What did you learn about the other person?

▶ Do you have the exact same values?

▶ Can you put the values you listed in order of importance for yourself? Why or why not?

Warm-Up Activity

❑ First you will need to write the word *agree* on a piece of paper and then write the word *disagree* on another piece of paper.

❑ Place those pieces of paper about twenty-five yards from you, directly next to each other.

❑ Use the rope to mark a starting point for this relay.

❑ Read the statements below one at a time.

❑ After you have read statement number one, each of you should run/walk/skip to the piece of paper that best describes whether you agree or disagree with the statement.

❏ Touch the paper with your hand and then run back to the rope.

❏ Do this until you have gone through all of the statements.
Statement 1: It is important to *always* tell the truth, no matter what.
Statement 2: You can judge what a person is like by the clothes they wear.
Statement 3: It is important to make a lot of money.
Statement 4: Parents are not as strict as they used to be.
Statement 5: We give off an impression of ourselves by the clothes that we wear.
Statement 6: It will be important for me to be married one day (if Adult is already married, statement might be, When I was a young girl, it was important for me to be married one day).

❏ When you are done, do some kind of energy award for each other. You can make one up or do a WOW.

Processing

▶ Did you agree on all of the statements?

▶ Go back through the statements and pick out two or three to discuss—especially ones that you disagreed on.

▶ Is it okay to disagree?

▶ Did you change your mind after hearing the other person's reasoning behind whether they agreed or disagreed with the statement?

▶ How did this activity make you feel? Did you like it or did it make you uncomfortable?

▶ Why are we afraid sometimes to discuss our differences of opinion?

Stretch

❏ For a list of stretches see the end of this chapter.

Workout

❏ Determine the lap distance you will cover. Mark the starting line with the rope.

❏ Today the goal is to try to cover three miles if possible and if time permits. Think of this as a practice 5K. We are now halfway through the ten-week program. You can walk, run, skip—just move forward for three miles, if you can.

❏ You may want to run together or separately.

❏ Place some paper and markers at the starting-line rope. While you are running/walking the three miles, think about what important values you possess that are motivating you to cover the distance. Maybe it's perseverance or self-discipline. Maybe encouragement or trying my best are others. If you want to write down a value when it crosses your mind, stop and do that at the starting point. If you want to wait until the end and write one or more down, you can do that, too.

Final Processing

▸ Look at the values you wrote down.

▸ Did any surprise you?

▸ How do you feel about your attempt to cover the three miles today?

▸ Are you happy with your performance or feeling something other than happiness?

▸ What values do you think are important for being a good athlete?

▸ What values do you think are important for being a good student?

▶ What values do you think are important for being a good friend and person?

▶ Take a few minutes to write down in your own journal what you learned today.

▶ Snap a photo of each other holding up your workout question sheet.

▶ Thought for the day: "Great Spirit, help me never to judge another until I have walked in his moccasins." (Sioux prayer)

▶ Give each other a hug and a high-five.

TWELVE: HELLO—ARE YOU IN THERE?

All About Good Listening Skills

Objective

1. To learn the essential elements of good listening
2. To practice the art of good listening
3. To differentiate between good listening and offering advice

Materials

❑ Paper
❑ Markers
❑ Rope for designating a starting point

Introduction

Either Girl or Adult reads the following out loud:

"Part of being a good friend, a helpful family member, and a cooperative colleague is being a good listener. Being a good listener takes work. There are actually three very important elements of being a good listener and we are going to learn those today."

Getting on Board

❏ Adult needs to read the following story to Girl. Girl needs to try to count the number of times the word *was* is said in the story. She has to listen really well to try to catch all of the *was*'s. She may not look over your shoulder as you read the story.

❏ Here is the story (start counting now): Once upon a time there **was** a girl named Molly. Molly loved to run. On a winter day, not too long ago, Molly **was** on a run in the city where she lived. She **was** running down a very busy four-lane street when suddenly she **was** surrounded by hundreds of dollar bills. It **was** very windy and the dollar bills were blowing all around her. She began to scoop up the dollar bills and soon discovered they weren't dollar bills, they were hundred-dollar bills. Molly **was** thrilled and then, as she scooped up the money, began to think about the person who actually lost the money. Then she came across a wallet. In the wallet **was** even more money. She picked up as many of the bills as she could and then she called the person who owned the wallet. The woman who owned it **was** so thankful. She **was** the treasurer for a church and **was** taking the collection from the Sunday service to the bank. She had left her wallet and the bag she carried the money in on top of her car and drove off. (She put it up there and forgot to take it off.) She **was** so happy when she saw Molly that she brought her some chocolate chip cookies.

Processing

Each of you should ask the other:

▶ How many times was the word *was* read in the story? (The correct answer is eleven.)

▶ What did you notice about trying to listen for the word *was*?

▶ Did you have to focus to listen for all of the *was*'s?

▶ Was that easy or difficult for you?

▶ Would it have been more difficult if you had been distracted by a lot of other noise or people around?

▶ What would have made it easier for you? Anything? If it was already easy, what made it easy for you to hear all of the *was*'s?

Warm-Up Activity

❏ Get out three pieces of blank paper.

❏ Write down the word *content* on one, *feelings* on another, and *values* on the last.

❏ These are the three important things you need to listen for when you are trying to be a good listener:

- **Content** is simply the facts of the situation or story. Good listeners simply repeat the story or situation back to the person. This is called paraphrasing. In the story above, you would simply repeat back what happened to Molly as she ran along the road.

- **Feelings** are what you try to listen for as the person tells the story. Listening to Molly's story, you might say, "Wow, it sounds like you were really happy at first about finding that money. But then you began to think about the person who lost it and you felt sorry for them. It sounds like you really wanted to return the money."

- **Values** are another thing you try to listen for as you are hearing the story. In response to Molly's story, you might say, "Molly, you are amazing. You found a lot of money—I mean a *lot* of money—and you valued honesty, respect, and the truth too much to keep it.

You gave it back to the person that it belonged to. That is awesome. You also respect yourself because you would have had to have lived with the dishonesty of keeping that when you actually knew who it belonged to."

❏ Place those three pieces of paper about fifty yards apart in a straight line. Place the starting-line rope fifty yards from the first one.

❏ At the starting-line rope, Girl needs to think of a recent situation that has bothered her at school. Maybe someone cheated off of her piece of paper or maybe a friend is doing something that hurts her feelings.

❏ She should take a few minutes and tell Adult the story.

❏ You both then run to the first piece of paper, Content. Adult should repeat the story back to Girl to make sure she understands the content of the story.

❏ Now you both run to the Feelings paper and Adult repeats to Girl what her feelings about the situation were.

❏ You then both run to the Values paper and Adult tries to get to the core value that Girl has discovered in the story she has told.

❏ Run back to the starting-line rope.

❏ When you are done, do some kind of energy award for each other. You can make one up or do a WOW.

Processing

▶ Did Adult get the three important elements of the story correct?

▶ If not, what did Girl do to make sure she got them correctly?

▶ Is part of good communication between two people taking the time to listen to each other?

▶ What is advice giving?

▶ Should we give advice when it isn't asked for?

▶ Why is it sometimes better to just listen?

Stretch

❏ For a list of stretches see the end of this chapter.

Workout

❏ Take a few minutes individually *before* the workout to think about a fun workout you would like to do today.

❏ Come back to each other and take turns sharing *your* idea of a fun run/walk workout for today.

❏ Between those two workouts, create one that takes into account the wishes for both of you.

❏ Now do that workout and *have fun*! Make sure to stop when you have about five minutes remaining in your session.

Final Processing

▶ How did each of you do, listening to each other's ideas?

▶ What is cooperation?

▶ Do we need to be good listeners to be able to cooperate?

▶ What was most fun about the workout?

▶ Were both of your wishes taken into consideration when you came up with the final workout?

▶ Take a few minutes to write down in your own journal what you learned today.

▶ Snap a photo of each other holding up your workout question sheet.

▶ Thought for the day: "The true sign of a friend is one who can listen to you with her heart, talk to you from her soul, and give a really good bear hug." (Molly Barker)

▶ Give each other a hug and a high-five.

THIRTEEN: THE IMPORTANCE OF COOPERATION

Objective

1. To explore what it means to be cooperative
2. To discuss the importance of getting along with others
3. To play out how cooperation can help us achieve our goals

Materials

❏ Three Dot-to-Dot worksheets (see pages 184 to 186)
❏ Paper
❏ Markers
❏ Rope for designating a starting point

Introduction

Either Girl or Adult reads the following out loud:

"Part of being a good friend means being able to cooperate. Let's take a minute and talk about cooperation. *Cooperation* means friends working together toward a common goal. When a person is on a soccer team, she has to cooperate so that the team can work toward the common goal of actually getting the ball in the goal! In our families, cooperation is necessary so that the house can run smoothly and we can get along."

Getting on Board

❏ This game requires your total concentration and can be dangerous if you aren't careful.
❏ First put a cone or beanbag about fifty yards away and use the rope to designate a starting point.
❏ On the count of three, Girl should take off running around the cone and back to the rope. Adult should time how long it takes.

- ❑ Now, Adult should untie her right shoe and Girl should untie her left shoe.
- ❑ Tie them together so that Adult's right foot is tied up right alongside Girl's left foot.
- ❑ Now on the count of three, the two of you should take off in three-legged fashion around the cone and back to the rope.
- ❑ Adult should time this effort, too.
- ❑ When you are done, untie yourselves from each other and tie your own shoe.

Processing

Each of you should ask the other:

- ▶ What was the difference in the amount of time it took to get around the cone solo and then tied together?
- ▶ Did you have to cooperate to get around the cone together?
- ▶ Does cooperation sometimes take time? Why do you think that? In other words did it take you longer to get around the cone tied together?
- ▶ Were you both trying to achieve a common goal of going around the cone? What about in the first effort? Were both of you trying to get around the cone or was just one of you?
- ▶ Doesn't it require more than one person to cooperate? Doesn't it make sense then that we need to cooperate with our friends?

Warm-Up Activity

- ❑ Label one of the Dot-to-Dot worksheets with Adult's name, another with Girl's name, and the third with no name.

❏ Place the starting line rope about twenty-five yards from a cone.

❏ Place the worksheets with your names on them at the cone.

❏ On the count of three, each of you should take off running from the starting line to the worksheets.

❏ On your first effort connect dot 1 to dot 2.

❏ Run back to the starting line, touch it, and then run back to the worksheet and connect dot 2 to dot 3.

❏ Continue running back to the starting line, touching it, and running to the worksheet connecting the dots one section at a time, until you have connected all the dots. (You should run for a total of ten times.)

❏ You can run/walk/skip this workout. But understand that each of you is operating independently of the other.

❏ Girl should remove the two labeled worksheets and put the blank one at the cone.

❏ Now, on the count of three, each of you start running together.

❏ You don't have to stay at the same pace or run next to each other.

❏ Run to the worksheet by the cone and connect dot 1 to dot 2. If you get there and that one is already connected, connect the next one in order. Then run back to the starting line and then continue running to the worksheet. You are simply connecting the next two dots in line.

❏ Both of you are working on the same worksheet.

❏ High-five each other when you have done the entire ten dots.

❏ When you are done, do some kind of energy award for each other. You can make one up or do a WOW.

Processing

▶ This time the result of the cooperation was a little different. Did you complete the worksheets faster together or when you had to complete them individually?

▶ Does cooperation sometimes help us reach our goal more efficiently and more quickly?

▶ What have you learned about cooperation so far today?

Stretch

❏ For a list of stretches see the end of this chapter.

Workout

❏ Today requires both of you to work your very hardest!

❏ Determine what your lap distance will be and designate the starting point with the rope.

❏ You are going to cooperate together today to cover three miles as quickly as you can.

❏ Create a baton by rolling up a piece of paper into a cylinder shape.

❏ Adult will time how long this activity takes.

❏ Girl will go first and run one lap.

❏ She will come around to the starting-line rope where Adult is waiting.

❏ She will hand the baton to Adult, who will then run a lap.

❏ Adult will return to the starting point and hand the baton to Girl.

❏ Continue taking turns completing the laps until you have covered three miles.

❏ This activity would be great on a real track that is at least a tenth of a mile.

❏ If you don't have access to one, estimate how many laps will make three miles.

❏ Now do that workout and *have fun*!

Final Processing

▶ How did you do as a team?

▶ Did you have to cooperate to make this workout work?

▶ Did you complete the three miles faster than if you had done it alone?

▶ Did you find that you worked a little harder knowing that someone was depending on you to do your best?

▶ What was the most fun about this workout?

▶ What have you learned about cooperation? Can it be fun? Does it bring us closer to the people we love?

▶ Take a few minutes to write down in your own journal what you learned today.

▶ Snap a photo of each other holding up your workout question sheet.

▶ Thought for the day: "Cooperation isn't always about making the goal, crossing the finish line, or scoring the point. Cooperation is about what we give of ourselves, accept from our friends, and learn in the process."
(Molly Barker)

▶ Give each other a hug and a high-five.

DOT-TO-DOT WORKSHEET
(Photocopy for easy use.)

1 .

. 2

3 .   . 4

5 .

. 6

7 .

8 .   .

10 .

DOT-TO-DOT WORKSHEET
(Photocopy for easy use.)

1 .

. 2

3 .   . 4

5 .

. 6

7 .

8 .   . 9

10 .

DOT-TO-DOT WORKSHEET
(Photocopy for easy use.)

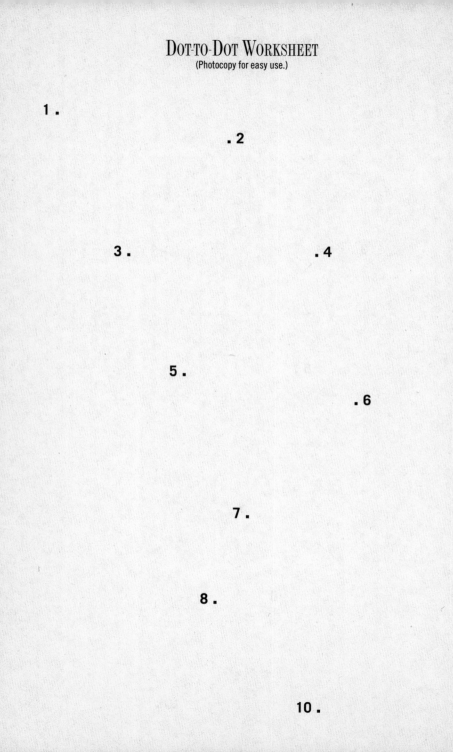

1 .

. 2

3 .

. 4

5 .

. 6

7 .

8 .

10 .

FOURTEEN: BODY TALK

The Messages We Give with Our Bodies, Our Voices, and Our Actions

Objective

1. To understand the messages we give using our bodies
2. To discuss the importance of matching our values to our body talk
3. Listening to our voices *and* our bodies

Materials

❏ Paper
❏ Markers
❏ Rope for designating a starting point
❏ Body Talk Questionnaire (see page 191)

Introduction

Either Girl or Adult reads the following out loud:

"One of the hardest concepts for people to understand is how we give off certain messages with our bodies. Body talk is a wonderful way to express the beauty that rests within—to show people who we are without using our voices. Yet our voices are also a wonderful way to express who we are—not with just *what* we say, but *how* we say it. Today we will be looking into how we can have our body talk match our values."

Getting on Board

❏ Take turns using body language to demonstrate the following concepts *without* using your voice: Confident; Stressed Out; Laid Back; Comfortable in One's Own Skin (Good Body Image); Negative View of Oneself; Positive Attitude.
❏ Now take turns using your voice to show the concepts below. Say the same phrase—*I'm a girl*—each time. For

example, the first time you say it, say it confidently.
Make sure your voice sounds confident.

❑ After voicing confidence, try voicing Stressed Out, Laid
Back, Negative View of Oneself, Positive Attitude,
Depressed, Happy.

Processing

Each of you should ask the other:

▸ Which body talk concept was the easiest to guess?

▸ Which voice was easiest to guess?

▸ Do we sometimes tell people a lot about us by how we
carry ourselves?

▸ What about our voices? Do they sometimes give away
what we are really feeling?

▸ Can you share with each other a time you wanted
others to think you were feeling one way, but your
body or voice gave away your true feelings?

Warm-Up Activity

❑ Take a minute with each other to review some of
the values you discussed in these past seven weeks.
Can each of you name a few of those? (Hint:
gratitude, self-respect, respect for others, acceptance,
open-mindedness, standing up for what we
believe in . . .)

❑ Mark the starting line for this relay with a rope.

❑ Girl should stand at the starting line.

❑ Adult should stand about twenty-five yards away with a
piece of paper and a pen.

❑ On the count of three, Girl should run to Adult and yell
out a value that she holds dear to her. Adult should
write that down on a piece of paper. Girl should run five
times, for a total of five values.

❑ Now switch places. Adult should be on starting line, run to Girl, and yell out a value she holds dear. It is okay if they possess some of the same values. Girl should write it down on a piece of paper. Adult should also run five times, for a total of five values.

❑ When you are done, do some kind of energy award for each other. You can make one up or do a WOW.

Processing

▶ Was it hard to remember some of the values you had discussed earlier?

▶ Did you think of any new values that you hadn't thought of before?

▶ Do we share similar values?

▶ What is one value that totally surprised you about me?

Stretch

❑ For a list of stretches see the end of this chapter.

Workout

❑ Today requires you to walk/run together.

❑ Determine the lap distance you will cover and use the rope to designate the starting point.

❑ Using the Body Talk Questionnaire on page 191, address the first value on Girl's list. While you are walking, answer the questions about body talk and expression of voice with regard to the value you possess.

❑ On the next lap, discuss the second value on your list. Use the questionnaire again to answer questions regarding body talk and voice expression.

❑ Because each of you listed five values, you should walk a total of ten laps today. If you would like to do more, go for it until your allotted time runs out!

Final Processing

▶ What did you learn about body talk and expression of voice?

▶ We have talked a lot about not judging a person by how he/she looks. What did you learn in this lesson?

▶ Is it important that we use all of our assets to convey the best person that we can be?

▶ Sometimes the way girls dress can be very confusing. What are some messages we give to others by the clothes we wear? Do we give off any messages at all about ourselves and what we believe in?

▶ How can we dress and use our body talk and our voices to show that we love and celebrate our body just as it is, without showing off too much of it?

▶ Name a movie star or model or anyone else in the public eye who you think gives off a negative message with her body talk and expression of voice.

▶ Now name a movie star or model or anyone else in the public eye who you think gives off a positive message with her body talk and expression of voice.

▶ Who are we more likely to see in magazines?

▶ Take a few minutes to write down in your own journal what you learned today.

▶ Snap a photo of each other holding up your workout question sheet.

▶ Thought for the day: "Look within! . . . the secret is inside you." (Hui-neng)

▶ Give each other a hug and a high-five.

BODY TALK QUESTIONNAIRE
(Photocopy for easy use.)

- The value we are discussing on this lap is [state it here].

- Does a person who possesses this value walk any particular way? If yes, demonstrate it for each other.

- Does a person who possesses this value have a certain tone in his/her voice? If yes, speak in that tone now.

- Does a person who possesses this value dress a certain way?

- Does a person who possesses this value act a certain way with her friends? If yes, how does she act?

- Does a person who possesses this value act a certain way at work/school? If yes, how does she act?

- After looking at all of the above questions, do you think we tell more with our bodies and voices than with the actual *content* of what we are saying?

- Give an example of where a person's content didn't match their body language or tone of voice. (A perfect example of this is the person who says "I'm *not* angry" in a very angry tone of voice, with arms crossed and fierce eyes.)

FIFTEEN: GOSSIP HURTS

How to Stop a Gossip Chain

Objective

1. To explore the negative effects of gossip
2. To explore ways we can *stop* a gossip chain
3. To understand how and why gossip starts

Materials

❏ Gossip Warm-Up Sheet (see page 196)
❏ Gossip Story (see page 197)
❏ Rope for designating a starting point
❏ Cones or beanbags to designate lap being covered

Introduction

Either Girl or Adult reads the following out loud:

"Today we will be talking about gossip. Gossip can really hurt a person's feelings and their credibility. Gossip serves no positive purpose. Most people gossip because they feel like they need to put others down to make themselves feel better. Today we will discuss what and how gossip starts and ways that you can stop a gossip chain."

Getting on Board

❏ Sit on the ground facing each other.
❏ Adult should read the following story to Girl: "Guess what I heard today. You know how Susan likes James. Well, today he stomped into her class, yelled at her to leave him alone, and then stomped back out. Susan started crying right there. Her teacher had to walk her to the counselor's office."
❏ Okay now read that story again, except this time go

back and replace "started crying" with "fainted."
Change "walk" to "carry."

❏ Now read it one last time and change the following
words: "class" to "house," "started crying" to "fainted,"
"teacher" to "father," "walk" to "carry" and "counselor's
office" to "hospital."

Processing

Each of you should ask the other:

▶ You only changed a few words. Did they change the
story?

▶ Did the story get more dramatic the more you changed
the words?

▶ Is this what happens with gossip?

▶ Can you see how the story can change each time a
person tells it?

Warm-Up Activity

❏ Taking the gossip warm-up sheet on page 196, cut out
each square and shuffle the cards.

❏ Place the cards at a cone that is about thirty yards
away from a starting line that you have marked with
your rope.

❏ On the count of three, Adult should run to the cone,
pick up one of the Gossip Warm-Up cards, and then
run back to Girl and tag her. Then Girl should run to
get a card.

❏ Continue until all of the cards have been picked up.

❏ Now take the cards and build a story with them. See
how dramatic you can make the story.

❏ When you are done, do some kind of energy award for
each other. You can make one up or do a WOW.

Processing

▸ Here is how the story was supposed to read: "Susan and James really like each other. The other day at school they were walking together to class. Susan's father came to school that day because he had signed up to do some volunteer work in the computer lab. He saw Susan and James. He ran over to Susan. He kissed her. She was so embarrassed. She asked him to never do that again in front of her friends. He was angry. He walked away."

▸ Was your story a lot more dramatic than the one described above?

▸ Is gossip usually more dramatic than what actually happened?

▸ Did you notice that not a single word was changed, just the order in which the sentences were placed?

▸ What have you learned about gossip?

▸ Why do you think people gossip?

Stretch

❏ For a list of stretches see the end of this chapter.

Workout

❏ Mark your starting point with the rope.

❏ You must run separately in today's workout.

❏ Take the Gossip Story on page 197 and place it at the starting point with a marker.

❏ When you complete a lap, read a sentence and then put a mark through it.

❏ Read the sentences in the numbered order on the page. If the sentence has been marked off, move to the next one.

❏ You should try to remember the content of each of the
sentences.
❏ Because there are twenty-four sentences, each of you
should try to run/walk about twelve laps.
❏ When you are all done, sit down together and try to
retell the story based on what you remember.

Final Processing

▶ Go back to the original Gossip Story and read it out
loud. How close was your story to the original?
▶ Did you make some mistakes?
▶ Do you think this is also how gossip might get started?
▶ If several girls were gossiping about someone else in
your class, what would you do?
▶ How can *you* stop a gossip chain?
▶ Take a few minutes to write down in your own journal
what you learned today.
▶ Snap a photo of each other holding up your workout
question sheet.
▶ Thought for the day: "May every word that you say be
said as if everyone in the world could hear it, for in fact
they can. May every wish that you wish another be a
wish that you wish for yourself, because in fact it is."
(Suze Orman)
▶ Give each other a hug and a high-five.

GOSSIP WARM-UP SHEET
(Photocopy for easy use.)

Susan and James really like each other.	The other day at school they were walking together to class.
Susan's father came to school that day because he had signed up to do some volunteer work in the computer lab.	He saw Susan and James.
He ran over to Susan.	He kissed her.
She was so embarrassed.	She asked him to never do that again in front of her friends.
He was angry.	He walked away.

GOSSIP STORY FOR WORKOUT

(Photocopy for easy use.)

1. There were two friends named Ashley and Britney.

2. They loved to go skating.

3. One day while they were skating, a speeding car nearly ran them over even though they were on the sidewalk.

4. Ashley and Britney were very frightened.

5. They skated a little farther down the road, when a police car came driving by.

6. The police car had its siren on.

7. The girls began to imagine all kinds of things about what was going on.

8. "Maybe the guys in that car are bank robbers and the police are chasing them," Ashley said.

9. "Maybe the guys in that car have escaped from jail and the police are chasing them," Britney added.

10. They skated a little farther down the road.

11. There on the side of the road was a huge canvas bag.

12. Britney stopped to look at it.

13. The bag had PROPERTY OF ACME BANK written on the side of it.

14. Britney leaned down to pick it up.

15. Ashley told her, "Stop—it might have something dangerous in it."

16. "What should we do?" Britney asked.

17. The girls decided to call the police.

18. They skated on down to the next convenience store.

19. They called the police from there.

20. The police came and got the bag that came from the bank.

21. And you might not believe this, but it had $100,000 in it.

22. The speeding car really *did* have bank robbers in it and the police really *were* chasing them.

23. Britney and Ashley were heroes.

24. They were honored by the mayor of their town.

SIXTEEN: BE POSITIVE IS NOT A BLOOD TYPE

The Importance of Having a Positive Attitude

Objective

1. To explore the powerful energy of positive thoughts
2. To introduce the concept of self-talk
3. To feel the difference between negative self-talk and positive self-talk

Materials

❏ Rope for designating a starting point
❏ Cones or beanbags to designate lap being covered

Introduction

Either Girl or Adult reads the following out loud:

"Today we will be talking about the importance of a positive attitude. People that have a positive and hopeful outlook on life tend to live longer, experience less stress, and have more meaningful and longer-lasting relationships. Having positive thoughts about ourselves is important to having a strong self-esteem. Today we will play a game that demonstrates the importance of having positive thoughts about ourselves and others."

Getting on Board

❏ Sit on the ground facing each other.
❏ Girl should start. Tell Adult what you want to be when you grow up. You should take two to three minutes to share your *biggest* dreams for what you want to be. You should hold *nothing back*.
❏ Adult, you need to be as supportive of Girl's comments as you can be. Don't judge or make any negative comments or facial expressions. Don't say, "Oh that's impossible," or, "That could never happen."

❏ Now Adult, you take about two minutes to do the same
with Girl. Tell her your biggest dreams for yourself, what
you would like to have in your life—it might not be job-
related but more about personal development or
something you would like to try but never have. Don't
hold back.

❏ Girl, you need to be as supportive of Adult's comments
as you can be. Don't judge or make any negative
comments or facial expressions. Don't say, "Oh that's
impossible," or, "That could never happen."

Processing

Each of you should ask the other:

▶ How did it feel to share these ideas with each other?

▶ How did it feel to listen and be totally supportive of
each other's thoughts?

▶ What do you think it would have felt like if one of you
had said to the other, "That's impossible," or "That
could never happen"?

Warm-Up Activity

❏ Place two cones fifty yards apart.

❏ Adult should stand at one cone and Girl at the other.

❏ On the count of three, Girl should take off, running
toward Adult. She may run, jog, or walk.

❏ Adult should cheer her on with all of her might. Scream
for her. "Go, Sally. Go. You are absolutely *awesome*. Keep
it up. You are amazing."

❏ When Girl gets to Adult, high-five each other.

❏ Now Girl should run back to her cone.

❏ When she gets there, Adult should take off, running
to Girl.

❏ This time Girl will cheer on Adult with all of her might.

❏ She should yell for her, scream, jump up and down, and encourage her with body and voice.

❏ When Adult gets to Girl, high-five each other.

❏ Adult, run back to your cone and repeat this process one more time!

❏ Have *fun* with it! Look silly, yell, scream, get excited.

❏ When you are done, do some kind of energy award for each other. You can make one up or do a WOW.

Processing

▶ How did it feel to encourage the other person?

▶ How did it feel to be encouraged?

▶ Which feels better, to *do* the encouraging or to *be* encouraged?

▶ If you are having a really rough day, what could you do to feel better based on what you learned today in this activity?

Stretch

❏ For a list of stretches see the end of this chapter.

Workout

❏ Mark your starting point with the rope.

❏ On the first lap, run separately. Don't make any eye contact. Don't talk to each other. Don't smile or even acknowledge the other person in any way.

❏ When you are done with that first lap, come back together and each read the following statement out loud. First Girl to Adult and then Adult to Girl: "You are so slow, can't you go any faster?" This feels really yucky, but try to do it anyway.

❏ Now run one more lap, without looking at or talking to each other. (I promise it gets better!)

❏ When you are done, read the following statement out
loud. Adult goes first and then Girl: "I am so slow. I
don't know why I even bother."

❏ Now run another lap, but this time when you see each
other, high-five each other, smile, yell, and cheer each
other on.

❏ When you have completed that lap, read the following
statement to each other (first Girl, then Adult): "You did
great. I am *so* glad you are my friend/mother/aunt/
father/daughter."

❏ Now do another lap in the same positive fashion. Enjoy
this lap. You can skip or hop—just have fun with it!

❏ When you are done, say the following statement out
loud (first Girl, then Adult): "I feel so good about my
body, my self, and what I just did."

❏ Continue running laps in this positive fashion. When
you have completed a lap, come up with positive
statements either about yourself or the other person.

❏ Continue until you have about ten minutes remaining
in your session.

Final Processing

▶ How did it feel the first two laps, when you were asked
to take on a negative attitude?

▶ Were the first two laps fun?

▶ How did it feel to make those negative statements
about the other person?

▶ How did it feel to make those negative statements about
yourself?

▶ Of the negative statements, which one was harder to say?

▶ How did it feel to run the laps with a positive attitude?

▶ Were the positive laps more fun? Did you have more
energy?

▶ How did it feel to make those positive statements about the other person?

▶ How did it feel to make those positive statements about yourself?

▶ Of the positive statements, which one was easier to say?

▶ Do we tend to say positive statements about others more often than we do about ourselves?

▶ Is it important to balance these?

▶ How do you feel right now, after having moved your bodies for an hour?

▶ Tell each other what you like most about having one-on-one time together.

▶ Take a few minutes to write down in your own journal what you learned today.

▶ Snap a photo of each other holding up your workout question sheet.

▶ Thought for the day: "Having a positive attitude is something I can choose."

▶ Give each other a hug and a high-five.

SEVENTEEN: PURPLE PEOPLE EATER

The Importance of *Not* People Pleasing and How to Stand Up for Yourself

Objective

1. To learn about the negative consequences of people pleasing
2. To differentiate between people pleasing and standing up for oneself
3. To differentiate between the need to be loved and feeling love

Materials

- ❏ Rope for designating a starting point
- ❏ Two large manila envelopes
- ❏ Markers
- ❏ Cone
- ❏ People-Pleasing Cards (from page 207)

Introduction

Either Girl or Adult reads the following out loud:

"Today we will be talking about the importance of standing up for oneself. Sometimes we are so afraid of hurting *other* people's feelings we might tell them what we think they want to hear. We do this in an effort to *not* hurt feelings. But usually when we don't tell the truth about ourselves and tell people what they want to hear instead of what is the truth about ourselves, we end up hurting feelings more. Sometimes we want so badly to be part of a group, to be popular, to be liked, or to be loved, we will do anything to get people to like us. This is called people pleasing. Today we will learn how to stop people pleasing and how to stand up for ourselves."

Getting on Board

- ❏ Understanding the difference between being loved and feeling love is important to understanding people pleasing.
- ❏ Girl should stand totally rigid with arms at her sides.
- ❏ Now Adult should walk up to her and embrace her, bear-hug her. Girl remains rigid. Hold that embrace for about thirty seconds.
- ❏ Now switch. Adult remains rigid and Girl bear-hugs her. Hold for thirty seconds.

❏ Now the two of you should bear-hug each other, both of you just hugging each other with all your might. Hold this for thirty seconds.

Processing

Each of you should ask the other:

▶ How did it feel to be hugged when you held your body rigid?

▶ How did it feel to hug the other person when they did not respond—when they were rigid?

▶ When you did the hugging, but it wasn't returned, how did it make you feel?

▶ Did you want to keep hugging until they hugged back?

▶ How was it different when the hug was mutual?

▶ When we are people pleasing, the relationship often feels one-sided, with one of us doing most of the work to sustain it. We keep doing things to *get* the other person to like us.

Warm-Up Activity

❏ Label one large manila envelope with the words *People Pleasing/Be Loved*.

❏ Label another large manila envelope with the words *Respect for Self and Others/Feeling Love*.

❏ Cut out the People-Pleasing Cards from page 207 and shuffle. Split the cards equally between the two of you.

❏ Place the starting-line rope on the ground and the two envelopes at a cone that is about thirty yards away.

❏ On the count of three, Adult should run one of her cards down to the appropriate envelope and place it inside.

❏ She then runs back and tags Girl. Girl takes off, running to place one of her cards in the appropriate envelope.

❏ You should run for a total of six times each.

❏ When you are done, do some kind of energy award for each other. You can make one up or do a WOW.

Processing

▶ Go through the envelopes. Did you get them right?

▶ As you go through the People-Pleasing envelope, are there any that you do that you would like to change?

▶ How about the Self-Respect envelope? Do you do any of those behaviors on a regular basis?

▶ What is the difference between wanting to be loved and feeling love? Which of these two motives is the healthier one?

Stretch

❏ For a list of stretches see the end of this chapter.

Workout

❏ Mark your starting point with the rope.

❏ Lay the cards from the warm-up next to the starting line.

❏ One very important way to *not* people please is to use the following assertive phrases: "I *feel* [state emotion here] *when you* [name the behavior the other person is doing that bothers you] *because* [tell the other person why it bothers you] *and I would like you to* [list the behavior here that you would rather have the person do]. For example, if your little sister keeps borrowing your clothes, instead of yelling at her or saying nothing (people pleasing) say, "Helen, I feel frustrated when you borrow my clothes without asking because I can't ever find what I want to wear. I would like for you to ask in the future. Okay?"

❏ Pick up one of the cards, and as you run the lap

together, discuss situations where you used either the positive, self-respecting behavior or the not-so-positive, people-pleasing behavior. If you get one of the people-pleasing behaviors, discuss what a more positive alternative would be. Perhaps using the *I feel*, *when you*, *because*, and *I would like you to* statements above would be a good alternative.

❑ You should complete at least twelve laps together.

Final Processing

▶ What do you think happens to a person if they always use people-pleasing behaviors?

▶ How does feeling love with someone make for a healthier relationship?

▶ What are ways that the two of you can enhance your relationship by feeling love?

▶ Adult, share with Girl one trait about *her* for which you are grateful.

▶ Girl, share with Adult one trait about *her* for which you are grateful.

▶ Take a few minutes to write down in your own journal what you learned today.

▶ Snap a photo of each other holding up your workout question sheet.

▶ Thought for the day: "Feeling love with others means being honest, having self-respect, and respect for others."

▶ Give each other a hug and a high-five.

PEOPLE-PLEASING CARDS
(Photocopy for easy use.)

Says yes to doing something even when she doesn't really have the time	Says no to doing something because she doesn't really have the time
Goes on crazy diets because she thinks if she gets thinner, more people will like her and she will be more popular	Eats in a healthy manner because it is good for her body
Lies about something she did because she is worried about hurting someone's feelings	Tells the truth to a friend about something she did, even if it might hurt her feelings
Gossips about a girl at your school so as not to feel left out	Stops a gossip chain by removing herself from the negative discussion
Has cosmetic surgery because she is trying to fit the picture of what a popular and pretty girl looks like	Loves her body just the way it is, because it is naturally beautiful and it is *her* body!
Smokes a cigarette because she is scared to stand up for herself and worried about what people will say about her if she doesn't	Turns down a cigarette because she knows what she believes in and doesn't *need* to smoke to be popular

EIGHTEEN: LETTING GO TO GROW

Letting Go of the People, Places, and Things
Over Which We Have No Control

Objective

1. To understand what it means to let go of people, places, and things
2. To understand that the only person over whom we really have control is ourselves
3. To understand that sometimes we can't control situations
4. To explore the relief that comes from letting go of the control we sometimes want to have over the actions of others

Materials

❏ A narrow 4-foot rod, such as a light curtain rod or tent pole—a broomstick would be too heavy
❏ Scissors
❏ Scenario cards (see page 212)
❏ Rope for designating a starting point

Introduction

Either Girl or Adult reads the following out loud:
"Today we will be learning all about letting go of those things in our life that we can't control. Sometimes we want things to happen so badly that we get all stressed out about them. But, you know, we can't control the traffic, the weather, the dog that ran away, or the person who didn't call us back. What we *can* control is our attitude about it and the thoughts we have about the situation. Consider the weather. To most of us, we don't like rainy days—they are inconvenient—we get wet—we can't play outside—and the traffic is usually worse. But now consider the construction worker. He might love a rainy day, because he can sleep in,

spend time with his children and watch a movie with his wife. We can always change our attitude about situations and people.

Getting on Board

- ❏ Adult and Girl should face each other, holding the rod between you.
- ❏ Adult should hold the rod up by letting the rod rest gently on the sides of her index fingers.
- ❏ Now Girl should put her index fingers under the rod, so it gently rests upon hers as well.
- ❏ On the count of three, gently lower the rod to the ground—*but the rod must always be touching all four index fingers.* If the rod is not resting upon all four index fingers, start over and do it again.
- ❏ Once you have successfully accomplished this, set up again the same way.
- ❏ Place the rod on all four index fingers and on the count of three, pull your index fingers away so the rod falls to the ground.

Processing

Each of you should ask the other:

- ▶ What happened when you tried to keep your fingers on the rod and *control* the action of lowering it?
- ▶ How many times did it take for you to lower it to the ground that way?
- ▶ What happened when you didn't try to control the action of lowering it and just removed your fingers and let it go on its own?
- ▶ How many times did it take for you to lower it to the ground when you just removed your index fingers?
- ▶ How does this relate to when we try to *control* the outcome of other people's actions?

▶ Have you ever noticed that if we try to control someone else, how they act, and the outcome of what they do, we get frustrated—and it generally takes longer or doesn't even happen?

▶ What happens if we let go of the outcome of others' actions but control ours?

▶ Do you think we will be healthier and happier if we don't try to control something we can't control?

Warm-Up Activity and Workout

❑ Today we are combining the warm-up and the workout to see how far you can go in the remaining time.

❑ You will be running/walking/skipping together.

❑ First, take the scissors and cut out the scenarios on page 212.

❑ Mark your starting place with the rope and place the scenarios in a stack next to it.

❑ When you start a lap, pick up a card and read the scenario. Each scene could potentially be a very frustrating situation, but think about a way you can change your attitude about it, so that you can let go of your frustration—your need to control the outcome. So that you can *go with the flow.*

❑ For example, if you had planned to go to an amusement park on Saturday, but woke up to find very rainy and cold weather. Typically, we might be very frustrated with this uncontrollable situation. But consider a different attitude. Maybe you can come up with a different activity that will be as much fun—or maybe you weren't supposed to go to the amusement park in the first place because you would have gotten a flat tire on the way. There is always a change you can make in your attitude to help better deal with the outcome of a potentially frustrating situation.

❑ Go as far as you can in the remaining amount of time. If you run out of scenario cards, think up real-life situations that have occurred in your life and discuss those.

❑ When you are done, do some kind of energy award for each other. You can make one up or do a WOW.

Final Processing

▶ What did you learn about trying to control things that are out of your control?

▶ What do you think happens to a person's stress levels if they are constantly trying to control situations and people?

▶ If you get really frustrated with a situation that's out of your control, do you think taking time to sit still, breathe deep, and consider a change in attitude will help calm you down?

▶ What is stress?

▶ Are stressed people often controlling people?

▶ Take a few minutes to write down in your own journal what you learned today.

▶ Snap a photo of each other holding up your workout question sheet.

▶ Thought for the day: "The beginning of love is to let those we love be perfectly themselves, and not to twist them to fit our own image." (Thomas Merton)

▶ Give each other a hug and a high-five.

SCENARIOS FOR DISCUSSION
(Photocopy for easy use.)

You planned to go to the local amusement park, but wake up to find torrential rains.	You have been invited to a party that you really, *really* want to go to and wake up that morning with a sore throat and fever.
You get a flat tire on the way to work.	Your best friend never returns your phone calls.
Your brand-new, favorite music CD is missing.	A friend of yours has started smoking and doing other behaviors that are *really* bad for her.
You left your handbag—with your credit cards, license, and cell phone in it—in a taxicab.	You get a really bad haircut.
You are training for your first 5K event and have put lots of time into it. Then you break your ankle.	You have applied for a job and discover that you are one of two finalists. You don't get the job.
Your husband/you/your father has lost his job and you are going to have to sell your house and move into an apartment.	Your best friend borrowed one of your favorite sweaters and lost it.
You have a very important appointment at 2:00. It's 1:45 and you are stuck in traffic.	Your best friend gets breast cancer.
A friend/boyfriend/husband gave you a beautiful diamond necklace and you've misplaced it.	Your best friend keeps making promises she doesn't keep.

NINETEEN: MAKING AMENDS

Learning to Say You're Sorry

Objective

1. To understand the importance of admitting when we are wrong
2. To learn how to make an amends
3. To prepare a list of people to whom we need to make amends and develop a plan on how to do that

Materials

- ❏ Paper
- ❏ Two pens
- ❏ Clipboard, if you have one
- ❏ Rope for designating a starting point

Introduction

Either Girl or Adult reads the following out loud:

"Today we will be discussing the importance of admitting when we are wrong. Sometimes it is very difficult to admit when we are wrong—we think that, somehow, by admitting that we are wrong, others may think we are dumb or won't respect us. One step beyond admitting we are wrong is making amends to the person we have harmed. When we have hurt someone, either unintentionally or intentionally, we usually know it. Walking around with this inside of us eats us up from the inside out. It is hard to look that person in the eye, and we may even go to extremes to avoid him or her. Eventually we begin to look for a way to avoid our feelings about this and we might even get sick, emotionally and physically. Today we are going to develop an action plan to clear our slate and make amends to those we have harmed."

Getting on Board

❑ Sit cross-legged and look at each other.

❑ Adult needs to share a story with Girl about a time when she hurt someone and she made amends to the person. Making amends is going one step further than saying sorry. Making amends includes *trying to make right what you have done wrong*. For example, if someone stole money from a place of work, they would actually return the money in addition to saying they were sorry. If you promised a friend you would do something for him or her and you didn't, you say you are sorry and then do it *now*, if it can still be done.

❑ Now, Girl should share a story where she hurt someone and then tried to make amends.

Processing

Each of you should ask the other:

▶ When we make amends, does it help us feel better about the situation?

▶ When we make amends, does it help us feel better about *ourselves*?

Warm-Up Activity and Workout

❑ Again, we are combining the warm-up and the workout. (See how we are running farther and farther with each lesson? Are you feeling stronger and better prepared for your 5K run?)

❑ Mark your starting point with the rope.

❑ Place several pieces of paper (on a clipboard, if you have one) and a couple of pens at the starting line.

❑ The two of you will walk/run/jog the workout together.

❑ Before you start, however, take a few minutes,

individually, to think of all the people in your past
that you have harmed but didn't settle things with.
Think of all the jobs you may have had where you
might not have been honest with your employer or a
time when you may have hurt someone's feelings. Try
to think of all of them. It may be helpful to think about
your life year by year, and consider where you were,
where you lived, what school you went to, the job you
held, etc.

❏ Now, write down one of those people whom you have
harmed on one of the pieces of paper. As you run the first
lap, talk to each other about that person. Discuss whether
it would be helpful to make amends to this person.
Would it actually be more harmful to them? You don't
want to make amends to make only yourself feel better. If
making amends will harm the other person, then you will
need to share what you did with each other and then
move on to another person you have harmed.

❏ Run/walk/jog the remaining amount of time.

❏ At the end of the workout you should have a list of
people to whom you might consider making amends.

❏ When you are done, do some kind of energy award for
each other. You can make one up or do a WOW.

Final Processing

▶ Sit down with each other.

▶ Look at the list of people you came up with.

▶ How do you plan to make amends to these people?

▶ Can you two set up a time where you can begin the
process?

▶ Does it require a phone call, a letter, or a meeting with
that person?

▶ How do you feel knowing that you soon won't have

these negative past behaviors resting inside you anymore?

▶ What do you think happens to people that hold all their mistakes inside?

▶ Do you respect people who can admit when they have done something wrong?

▶ Take a few minutes to write down in your own journal what you learned today.

▶ Snap a photo of each other holding up your workout question sheet.

▶ Thought for the day: "He who would have beautiful roses in his garden must have beautiful roses in his heart." (S. R. Hole)

▶ Give each other a hug and a high-five.

TWENTY: SHARING OUR LOVE FOR EACH OTHER

Objective

1. To provide closure to the ten weeks together
2. To review what we have learned
3. To affirm *just how much we love each other*

Materials

❏ Rope for designating a starting point
❏ Paper
❏ Two markers
❏ One cone

Introduction

Either Girl or Adult reads the following out loud:

"Today is our last day. Can you believe it? We have come so far. We can now run farther than we ever could, we know each other so much better, and we feel a *ton* better about ourselves. Today we are going to go over some of the things we learned and just celebrate each other. We might feel a little sad. We might feel overjoyed at what we've accomplished. It's okay. Whatever we are feeling, we are just going to let it flow!"

Getting on Board

❏ Sit cross-legged and take each other's hands.

❏ Talk about love for a minute. Don't have any expectation, but simply answer the questions, What is love? and What does love feel like?

Processing

Each of you should ask the other:

▶ How are you feeling right now?

▶ Are you a little sad?

▶ What do you want to say about the experience you've had over the last ten weeks?

Warm-Up Activity

❏ Mark your starting point with the rope.

❏ Take two pieces of paper. At the top of one put Adult's name. At the top of the other, put Girl's.

❏ Place those pieces of paper about thirty yards away from the starting-line rope. Mark them with a cone. If it's windy, put a beanbag or a rock on the pieces of paper. You could also use a clipboard to hold them in place.

❏ On the count of three, both of you take off running from the rope to the cone.

❏ On the piece of paper with Girl's name, Adult should write one thing she loves about her.

❏ Girl should do the same on Adult's paper.

❏ You both should return to the rope, touch it with your

hand, and run back to the cone and mark down more positive words about the other person.

❏ Continue doing this until each of you has run six times.

❏ When you are done, do some kind of energy award for each other. You can make one up or do a WOW.

Processing

▶ Get the pieces of paper.

▶ Adult should hold Girl's paper and Girl should hold Adult's paper.

▶ Adult first reads out loud to the girl. "I love _____." She should read each thing she loves about the girl and make sure to put the "I love" in front of each thing she says.

▶ Now Girl does the same thing for Adult.

▶ Did anything the other person said surprise you?

▶ Remember how we talked about being loved, as opposed to feeling love? Are you *feeling* love right now?

▶ What does feeling love feel like?

Stretch

❏ For a list of stretches see the end of this chapter.

Workout

❏ Here is a list of the lessons we have covered. For each lap you walk/run/jog, talk about one of the lessons. It might be easiest to do the lessons in order.

❏ If you can, discuss how what you learned in that lesson helps us *feel* love with ourselves and with others.

WEEK ONE:

Lesson One: Getting to Know Each Other

Lesson Two: Making Promises to Each Other

WEEK TWO:

Lesson Three: Taking My Own Inventory: Assessing My Current Set of Needs, Wants, and Habits

Lesson Four: Let's Get Physical: Being Physically Healthy

WEEK THREE:

Lesson Five: It's Okay to Be Emotional: Being Emotionally Healthy

Lesson Six: It's Cool to Be Myself

WEEK FOUR:

Lesson Seven: Finding the Spirit in Me: Being Spiritually Healthy

Lesson Eight: Life's Balance Beam: Maintaining Balance in a Crazy World

WEEK FIVE:

Lesson Nine: Life Is the Ultimate Rush: Steering Clear of Tobacco, Alcohol, and Other Drugs

Lesson Ten: Beauty Is an Inside Job: Avoiding Eating Disorders

WEEK SIX:

Lesson Eleven: I Believe . . . What Do I Believe, Anyway?

Lesson Twelve: Hello—Are You in There? All About Good Listening Skills

WEEK SEVEN:

Lesson Thirteen: The Importance of Cooperation

Lesson Fourteen: Body Talk: The Messages We Give with Our Bodies, Our Voices, and Our Actions

WEEK EIGHT:

Lesson Fifteen: Gossip Hurts: How to Stop a Gossip Chain
Lesson Sixteen: Be Positive Is Not a Blood Type: The Importance of Having a Positive Attitude

WEEK NINE:

Lesson Seventeen: Purple People Eater: The Importance of *Not* People Pleasing and How to Stand Up for Yourself
Lesson Eighteen: Letting Go to Grow: Letting Go of the People, Places, and Things Over Which We Have No Control

WEEK TEN:

Lesson Nineteen: Making Amends: Learning to Say You're Sorry
Lesson Twenty: Sharing Our Love for Each Other

Final Processing

▶ Lie down next to each other.
▶ Lie in the silence. Hold each other's hands if you like.
▶ Stay quiet for five minutes. (You can set a timer if you want.) Look up at the sky or close your eyes.
▶ Take time to be totally present in the moment and feel whatever it is you are feeling.
▶ Sit up after five minutes.
▶ Sit cross-legged across from each other and take each other's hands.
▶ Say whatever you want to say.
▶ Take a few minutes to write down in your own journal what you learned today.
▶ Snap a photo of each other holding up your workout question sheet.

▶ Thought for the day: "Remind me each day that the race is not always to the swift; that there is more to life than increasing its speed. Let me look upward into the towering oak and know that it grew great and strong because it grew slowly and well." (Orin L. Crain)
▶ Give each other a hug and a high-five.

SOME IMPORTANT TIPS ON STRETCHING

There are many benefits to stretching. Stretching
▶ Maintains and increases range of motion
▶ Decreases risk of injury
▶ Lessens muscle tension and fatigue
▶ Lessens or prevents muscle soreness after a workout

Never bounce when stretching. This actually causes the muscle you are trying to stretch to contract. Stretch to the point of mild tension, and hold ten to thirty seconds. The following stretches, except that for the outer thigh/hip, are to be done *standing up* for ease of use in any setting.

UPPER BODY STRETCHES

Shoulders
❏ Standing, clasp hands and stretch arms above head.
❏ Place right hand behind shoulders with elbow directed upward. Grab elbow with other hand and gently pull toward your head. Repeat on opposite side.
❏ Keeping back straight and shoulders relaxed, clasp hands

behind hips. Exhale and gently lift hands and arms as
one unit.

Lower Back

❏ With legs shoulder-width apart, lean over with hands on
thighs just above the knees. Arch back up to the sky,
keep head down. Now reverse the stretch by lifting head
and buttocks upward (like "cat" and "dog" poses in
yoga).

LOWER BODY STRETCHES

Quadriceps

❏ Using a wall or fence for balance, grab right foot with
right hand, gently pulling it behind you by bending the
knee. Keep the angle slightly open.

Hamstrings

❏ Stand facing a tree, fence, or bench and elevate one leg
onto the object. Slowly bend forward at the waist until a
stretch is felt in the back of the elevated leg, keeping
both knees slightly bent. Repeat with the other leg.

Inner Thigh

❏ Stand with feet apart, just beyond shoulder width. With
hands on hips and torso upright, squat down so that
knees bend outward until stretch is felt.

Outer Thigh/Hip

❏ Sit with right leg extended in front of you. Pull left knee

into and across chest toward opposite shoulder. Repeat
opposite leg.

Calf and Ankle

❏ Lean into a wall or fence with one foot in front of the
other. Back foot points straight ahead. All weight
forward, pressing back heel to floor. Hold. Then slightly
bend back knee, hold. Repeat with other leg.

SIX

GETTING READY FOR YOUR FIRST 5K

So now you've gone through the ten-week program and you are signed up for your first 5K running event. All of your physical efforts over the last ten weeks are about to come full circle as you celebrate the absolutely *amazing* body that you have been given.

Some of you may have run a 5K before. Others of you may have never run a step in your life before starting this program.

Let's review some important aspects of getting ready for the race in the bigger picture and then the specifics of race-day preparation.

Ideally, you have chosen a race that falls almost immediately after you have completed the ten-week program. You may have noticed how the workouts got longer and longer and the warm-ups got shorter. The reasoning behind this is to slowly increase your cardiovascular conditioning over the ten-week period so that by race day, you are primed.

So let's review everything you will need to know to be ready.

CLOTHING

What is the predicted temperature on race day? Are you expecting cold weather, very hot weather, high winds, rain? Being prepared for a variety of conditions is important, but having a close estimate of what weather to expect will help you limit the number of clothing options you take to the race.

If the weather is very cold, make sure to dress with layers of clothing rather than one huge bulky piece of clothing. Layered clothing will allow you to take off unneeded clothing as your body temperature increases, during the run itself. Believe it or not, the clothing you choose for after the race is as important as during the event itself. During the event, as expected, your body temperature goes up and you will undoubtedly sweat a little bit (or if you are like me, a lot, even in the coldest of conditions). Immediately after the race, try to take off all sweaty clothing and put on dry warm clothing. Your body temperature will drop quickly and uncomfortably if you are underdressed and damp after an event.

If the weather is extremely hot, dress as lightly as possible. If you are comfortable running in only a small top and running shorts, go for it! The less clothing on your body, the cooler it will stay.

Don't forget the importance of taking care of your feet during the race. Wear socks that wick water away from the surface of your feet. Socks made of cotton, although they may be comfortable, are not conducive to running and will likely produce painful blisters on your feet. There are a number of brands on the market that are specifically made for running. (DeFeet is an excellent brand and comes with fun colors and designs—my favorite is Girls Love Dirt.)

Remember how we talked about shoes earlier? Now is *not* the time to buy new shoes. You are better off wearing an old pair than hoping for the magic powers of new running shoes. New running shoes take at least two good weeks to be worn in and may actually cause foot pain on a first run. You don't want this to happen during your first 5K.

Another essential piece of clothing is an extra-supportive bra. This can make all the difference between a comfortable and uncomfortable experience. Even those of us with very small breasts need to get a supportive running bra. You can purchase these at most sporting good stores, specialty running stores, and even some large department store chains.

NUTRITION

For a short event, like a 5K, don't change anything about your diet the week or day before the race. Hopefully, you already eat a fairly healthy diet, so no need to carbo-load, protein-deprive, or make any other kind of wacky nutritional adjustments to prepare for the 5K.

Having a small meal race morning is critical to having a good race. Going into a race ravenous guarantees a poor performance. However, going into the race with a full stomach guarantees cramps. A happy medium is to eat two to three hours before the race starts. I usually have a banana, a cup of coffee, and a PowerBar. There are many energy bars on the market. Find one that suits your palate and your digestive system.

Most races provide a cornucopia of goodies at the finish line. Indulge. Celebrate. Partake. Your body needs to replenish what fuel and liquids it lost during your running effort. Don't overindulge, but make sure to eat foods high in carbohydrates and minerals. A whole-wheat bagel and some fruit is ideal.

Water is essential, however. Make sure to drink water if you are thirsty before the event—but not immediately before the race or you may get stomach cramps. Recent research shows that you can overhydrate—which, ironically, dehydrates your body. So the week, day, and hours before the race, drink *when you are thirsty*. No need to drink any more water than usual.

You may want to take in some water during the race if it is very hot. Most 5K runs have a water aid station approximately halfway through the course. Running and drinking at the same time is a real art. Feel free to stroll through the aid station, drink part of the water, and take the rest and throw it on your head. Cooling off the inside *and* outside of your body is critical in very hot temperatures.

SLEEP

Sleep is another critical factor in having a good race/run performance. But don't expect to get a great night's sleep the night before the race. Usually you'll be a little nervous, excited, and, if you are well-hydrated, heading to the bathroom a couple of times. So just expect to wake up early, jazzed to go. What you can try to do to compensate for a poor night of sleep the night before the race is to get a *great* night's sleep the two nights prior to that. I have personally found the night immediately before the race more important for preparing my body and mind for the race.

WHAT RACE DAY LOOKS LIKE

You'll probably wake up early. You will be excited. You will more than likely set your alarm for a few hours before the start time and still wake up before it rings.

Grab some breakfast. Eat lightly. A little coffee may be

beneficial in giving you a bit of a boost to start the day. But don't overindulge on the coffee. The brown stuff is a diuretic and will have you dehydrated before the start of the race and may even cause diarrhea.

Get to the race about one hour before start time. Take into account parking—is this a well-known, well-attended race where parking could be an issue? Consider parking in a space that will allow you to go home immediately after the race is over. If you park anywhere near the racecourse, your car may be trapped by road closures and other safety issues until every finisher has completed the event.

There will be lots of people and are usually very few Porta-Johns. Because of the increased nervous stimulation (remember how excited you are about the race?) you will more than likely make several trips to the bathroom. You may even wonder if you have a sick stomach—diarrhea is a common before-race response. Do your best to eliminate your bladder and bowels before the start of the race. Trying to run with an overfilled digestive system causes cramps, is uncomfortable, and will eventually take all your willpower to keep it from eliminating on its own during the race. So go to the bathroom as often as is necessary to become a lean, mean, fast machine!

If you haven't preregistered, you can usually register the morning of the event. At registration you will be handed a goody bag full of freebies and pieces of literature provided by the event's corporate sponsors. You will also find your race number and some safety pins. Pin your race number to the front of whatever you plan to wear during the entire race. Because I tend to heat up pretty quickly and remove some articles of clothing as I run, I usually pin my number to my shorts—which I definitely don't plan to shed during the race!

Folks should start lining up for the race about five to ten

minutes before start time. The five-minute-mile runners will be on the front of the starting line and runners usually seed themselves voluntarily according to an estimated run time. If you don't know where to position yourself ask someone near you where you should start. Runners are generally the nicest, most inclusive group of athletes in the world. Let them know this is your first race. You will be warmly welcomed into the fraternal order of runners and more than likely escorted to a proper position.

Many races use a "timing chip" system. You will need to determine if this is the type of system being used at your event. The chip enables organizers to get the exact time it took you to cover the course. In other words, your official time will not begin with the firing of the starting gun, but when you actually cross the starting line. Your time when you cross the finish line is also captured on the chip, and your exact running time is then calculated with a device used by the race organizers. You will receive your chip at the time of registration. The chip is tied to your shoe using your shoelaces. Be sure to tie it firmly to the top of your shoe. If it comes off you have to pay for the chip *and* you will not receive a time for the event.

The chip system is wonderful in larger races. I competed in the Chicago Marathon a couple of years ago. At that time it was the largest marathon in the United States. It took me more than three minutes just to cross the starting line. If we hadn't used chips, I would have been timed from the sound of the gun and my official time would have been nearly four minutes more.

Two to three minutes before the gun goes off, people start cheering, clapping, jumping up and down, and doing last-minute stretches. This is when the fun begins. When that gun goes off, many of the runners will take off too quickly. A very large portion of those "rabbits" will slow down dramatically after a few hundred yards. I would encourage you—particularly if it is your first race—to start out slow and increase your speed throughout the 5K.

Be sure to pace yourself. Let your breathing get into perfect sync with your steps. Try not to be swayed by the pace of those around you. Do what you need to do to enjoy *and* finish the event.

Festivities before and after the event are fun and in many instances entertaining. Good food, good music, and lots of celebrating occur after the race is completed. If you can stick around for a while after you've finished, do. You will meet lots of runners, make new friends, and really begin to feel a part of your local running community.

Festivities include an awards ceremony. Most events break racers up into age-group categories in five-year increments. If you are an older runner or a much younger runner, you may discover that you have won an award. These age-group categories often don't have a lot of participants, so you can go home with some winner's loot! Race times, too, are usually posted at the awards ceremony. You can walk away knowing the exact time it took you to complete the course.

You may discover, several hours after the race, that you are either jubilant and full of energy or a little depressed and extremely tired. People seem to fall into one of those two categories. The depression may result from your body being tired and the "party's over" letdown of having accomplished the goal for which you've been training. Others may feel totally light on their feet and ready to conquer the world. You have just finished your first 5K and you can do anything.

Be careful not to jump back into heavy and hard training right away. Your body will need a day to recuperate and rebuild tired muscles.

Enjoy the fruits of your labor. Relax a little and consider going for a hike on the next few weekends—enjoy your newfound fitness in activities other than running. You might try a bike ride, swimming, or a slightly longer running event in the weeks to come. Celebrate all the amazing wonders of your body. Consider the fact that you are in a small minority of people that can run 3.1 miles. Let the confidence of having completed this wash over you when you walk into a roomful of strangers. Hold on to that as you attempt to set new goals at work or in school. Consider the risk you took to complete this 5K the next time you want to risk a little of yourself in a relationship.

Amy Kattwinkel, a local elite runner, qualified for the Olympic Trials in the marathon several years ago. I remember talking to her in the locker room, not long after she'd finished the Trials. "What do you think about during that distance? How do you stay focused?" I asked her. She replied, "All I could think about as the miles ticked down was, 'Darn, I've only got thirteen more miles to go. . . . Now I've only got nine miles to go. . . . Oh no, only three miles to go.' " I was astounded at her response. Most of us would have thought, *Oh my gosh, I've got thirteen more miles to go!* Or *I'm so tired and I still have four miles to go,* or *When will this ever end?* Amy was wishing for more. Her love of running and her desire to experience every moment of the event filled her with gratitude, wonder, and appreciation.

Now that I'm in my forties, I've started to view my life in this manner. When I was younger, I never thought I would get older. Sixteen and a driver's license seemed so far away. The independence of college life was out of reach. The world of the grown-up was inaccessible. But now, I am counting down the miles that stretch before me and on some level, saddened that they are decreasing.

Today, Helen worked really hard to frustrate me at a restaurant. Her misbehavior landed her in four minutes of time-out when we got home. "But Mommeeeeeeeeee," she wailed. "Four minutes is sooooooooooo long."

Four minutes multiplied by years makes up a lifetime. In the blink of an eye, my little girl will be all grown-up. I often catch myself feeling such sorrow as the minutes of my life pass before me. I embrace the minutes that I have, but I also mourn their passing. I treasure the times when my children do something that expands their independence, but weep at the disappearance of their youth.

Oh, how quickly they grow. Wasn't it just yesterday that my son lay in my arms, an infant, helpless, the two of us focused only on each other? Wasn't it just yesterday he smiled his first smile, took his first step? And now he is my strapping seven-year-old who talks about the gravity in black holes and the first astronaut on the moon. He is the little man who comforts his sister at night, fixes his own lunch, and carries on intellectual discussions such as, "How long has God been around, anyway?"

I now run each step of my life looking at the process—not the finish line. I examine the bricks of time that rest beneath my feet. I welcome each advancing step while I wave good-bye to those behind me. I'm embracing my life while letting it go. I joyously cling to the experiences that make up my life and at the same time feel such sorrow as they slip through my fingers.

I've run half my life's race at this point. I plan to savor every step of it, from here to the finish line.

You are about to run your first 5K. What will the experience mean to you?

SEVEN

WHEN MOTHERS RULE THE WORLD

I'm in an airplane as I write this, returning from an emotional weekend at my older sister's wedding. This is her second marriage. Emily wasn't around for much of my growing-up years. She is thirteen years older than I am and she was out of the house by the time I was four.

She didn't weather the storm of my mother's alcoholism like my sister Helen and I did. But Emily weathered her own storms. The middle child, in between two very outgoing children, Emily is the artist in our family. She is a dancer, poet, writer, and an immensely spiritual person.

I watched her and her new husband recite their vows to one another. She is fifty-five; he is sixty-seven. They peered into the landscape of each other's eyes as they said their vows privately to each other and publicly before dozens of their friends.

I felt a strange mix of joy and sorrow. Joy that the sister who had hidden in her own shadows of despair for so long—who had buried herself deep in the Girl Box to escape her first, and very painful, marriage—had found her soul mate. He is a man whom she adores and with whom she can at last share her whole self.

My sorrow comes from my own longing to find that comfort—first with myself and then with someone like her husband, David. Someone who is warm, compassionate, gentle, and understanding. I long for the depth of friendship that comes with age, that matures like a fine wine; in which beauty lies not only in the way we speak to each other but in how we mutually admire the character lines in each other's faces, reflecting the years of living that will one day drape our skin across our bones like folds of velvet fabric. I yearn for the touch of rough hands that will hold mine on long walks. Rough hands with fingers that will delicately trace the veins upon my old hands while we sip coffee and talk into the black liquid of night.

The year it has taken to write this book has been a challenging one. Any wish of recovering my marriage—the small flame of hope I had fanned and protected—has been blown out by the wind of indifference. My mother—*my best friend*—died and left a hole so deep, I'm still seeking the light outside of the black despair. Moving into a house and taking on all the responsibilities that come with it; the ever-increasing adult demands; my children growing up; and the challenges of single motherhood and the guilt that comes with feeling that I always need to be in two places at the same time. My life has, on many levels, felt chaotic and out of control.

I'm not alone in that swirling mass of chaos and worry. Women carry the burden of the world upon our shoulders.

I remember the days on which my children were born: the

first time I held my son—and, three years later, my daughter—
the depth of that love; how they nursed so naturally. I felt as if I
had one foot on earth and the other in heaven. Their births
were an amalgam of joy and pain, celebration and fear.

The gift of motherhood has been a glorious one. I see the
world in a completely different way.

I can't look at a crying child anymore and not feel the pain
of his tears—my arms long to reach out and rock his little-boy
body to sleep.

I cannot watch the advertisements on TV that depict the
bloated bellies of doe-eyed children in Third World countries,
of children who are tired of crying, longing, yearning, starving
to death.

I can't tolerate the stories of children beaten, left in basements and closets, burned, broken, and abused, their helpless
little lives cowering away while wishing—wishing for one gentle touch, one small hug, one small kernel of love.

I can't bear to know that little boys and girls shake with fear
in the basements of their homes while bombs explode like
Fourth of July fireworks and the angry chants of war rage all
around them.

I simply can't take the unacknowledged fear and anger of a
little boy and girl who wonder if Daddy will stop drinking this
time, if the stench of beer on his breath will be absent this
night when he puts them to bed.

I weep to learn of women in burkas who see the world
through black veils, who must stay silent with each step, who
must live in darkness; women who never know the sweet touch
of a child's hand across their face or the wind's caress across
their body or the warmth of the sun upon their skin.

I am appalled at the life of the battered woman who at last
finds reprieve in a shelter with her two children. She is thrilled
with her newfound strength—enough strength now to hold a

job. She is thrilled to make minimum wage as long as she's on her own, away from her abuser. Meanwhile, CEOs across America are skimming money off the top and spending hundreds of thousands of dollars on the toilets in their billion-dollar homes.

I simply cannot take it anymore. I simply *won't* take it anymore.

Chloe is one of my best friends. She is nine years old. The last time I saw her, she ran up to me. "Look Molly. Look!" She showed me the sparkles across her fingernails—the silver glitter of girlhood. She was proud of the adornment, thrilled by the simplicity of it.

I admired those ten fingers—every one of them. Each finger is different—each finger a celebration of glitter, the result of a holiday manicure with her grandma.

I took her little hands in mine and I praised them— awestruck at what these two little hands would create in her lifetime.

I look at my own hands and the splendor there: the telltale signs of age in the raised veins, liver spots, and wrinkles.

These hands of mine have done much in their lifetime.

The little-girl hands that molded clay ashtrays at summer camp, which my father proudly displayed at his office. "My daughter made this. Isn't it beautiful?"

The girl-hands that delighted in holding a boy's hand for the first time, hands that later that night pressed on his lower back as our young bodies slow-danced: the tender touch, the tender moment, this tender memory.

The hands of a young woman exploring her own sexuality and the discovery there—*down there*—of the layers of my wom-anness: the pleasure, the sensation, the wonder of it all. The same hands that ignited the passion in another, that first touch, that first innocent expression of first love. The power of it. So frightening and wonderful at the same time.

The wife-hands that comforted a depressed and weeping husband, that held his shaking body, brushed back the stray strands of hair from his face; the empty hands that desperately yearned for his touch in return.

The mother-hands that held my babies while they nursed, changed diapers at three in the morning, gently washed baby skin, and touched their tiny toes and delicate fingers; hands that played this little piggy, untangled hair, and blew kisses as they marched off to their first days of kindergarten.

The healing hands that placed Band-Aids on skinned knees and provided magical powers on hurt places.

The weathered hands that wash dishes, mend clothes, do yard work, clean house, and fold laundry.

The loving hands that reach out to my children in those peaceful moments when we interlock our fingers and sit in the still of the moment.

The hands of despair that lift to the sky, gesturing hopelessness, rage, and fury.

The hands of hope that come back down again—in prayer.

Women's hands have much to offer. Our hands gently and lovingly sew the tapestry of our lives, each delicate stitch of which carefully holds together the lives of so many others.

Our world is in turmoil. But I am convinced that we can change all that. Although women don't yet hold as many of the positions we typically call powerful—CEO, president, politician, world leader—I am certain that we can influence the world order.

We can teach our sons, husbands, and fathers the wonder of compassion—the strength of love versus defense. We can help them to see the world through our eyes—the eyes of the mother.

We can ask our sons, husbands, and fathers to hold their own babies. Ask them to look their babies in the eyes and honestly tell them that war works. Can he ask his child to suffer at the hands of war—to kill and possibly be killed? Or can he embrace his child and assure her that peace will come to those who believe in it, peace will come to those who give it away, peace will come to those who love.

We can ask our sons, husbands, and fathers to hold their enemy's babies—to lift them up for slaughter. Can he hold that innocent child in his arms and tell her that her life is unimportant, worth sacrificing for *our* cause? Or can he hold her as if she were his own, assure her that peace will prevail, that she is loved and worthwhile, no matter what?

We can ask the men in our lives to look into the eyes of a child as he cries for the touch of his dead father—our "enemy"—whose body lies still on the dry dirt.

We can ask our husbands to hold the crying and terrified child of a battered woman.

We can ask our fathers to tuck their own children into bed at night and imagine the burns and bruises on countless other children who have never known the gentle touch of their own father—only his rage after too much drinking.

Women's hands are powerful. We know the world through what our hands feel, embrace, and love. We build our lives on relationships, take time to touch our children, hug our neighbor, and reach out to others. We are in the "global trenches"—the frontline—working one-on-one with one another and with children. We hold our crying babies, relate to their fear, and constantly reassure in spite of the chaos around us.

We need to take the hands of our lovers, our sons, and our fathers and walk them gently into our world. Show them the wonder of motherhood, the universal and immediate connection we feel with our sisters whether we live in the United States, Iraq, or any other part of the world. The women of the world need to take the hands of their husbands and sons and softly place them on the first kicks of our growing babies and marvel at the life there.

We need to walk them through the halls of our lives, through the countless hours we spend nurturing little broken hearts and hurt feelings. We need to gently take their hands in ours and coach them in the artistry of molding anger into growth and revenge into forgiveness.

I love to sit in the steam room. I haven't been in there for months, so today after a cold run in damp winter rain, I lay down on the marble bench and felt the steam fall down over my body like the humid Southern summer.

I listened to the surge of steam as it escaped the valves that restrained it, unleashing the burst in a violent start that settled into a steady stream of noise and heat, followed by the sudden quiet as it shut down, refueling for the next surge.

I love the violent quiet of the steam room—the solitude, the comfort to my aching bones after a bike ride or run. The pleasure of sweat through pores and the tickle of it as it runs down my skin. I love to lie in the wonder of my own body and give thanks to God, there in the steam room, in my sanctuary.

I do a lot of thinking in the steam room.

And today I had a vision. A vision of such intensity that ' would call the moment an awakening.

Mothers need to rule the world.

Mothers need to rule the world.

It is time for mothers to do something—to our gentle and loving ways to say enough

It's time to lay bare Woman's vie nally release from our womb this umbilicus and let her learn to unsure at first, but with growing the gentle hands of love and caring, midwife, we need to lift *our* world and *our* vision from the womb of *our* knowing and transition her into this new world—a world we can create, a world we can transform.

Our feminine spirit can powerfully transition that child—that vision—from one world to another. Like a river that flows through varying terrain, we can carry our world through tears, longing, confusion, pain, and sorrow to strength, joy, understanding, forgiveness, and love.

Women are a place of warmth and sanctuary. We hold the power of the womb where babies are born and passion is found. It is here in the confines of our physical bodies that something mysterious, holy, and glorious occurs. We incubate babies and nourish souls. We learn the true meaning of unconditional love.

And now it is time to share that unconditional love, that vision—our undying belief in the goodness of people—with those around us. I encourage the women of the world to hold the hands of our lovers, our fathers, our sons, drink coffee with them and talk into the black of night. To trace lines of love on veins of age while we talk about things that really matter—like children, compassion, life, peace, and love. We can run for office, lead a corporation and wear a suit and still hold on to our mother-self, tender viewpoints, and feminine perspective. We can be mothers, teachers, social workers, and nurses and still be assertive.

We need to realize the power that resides in us and use it.

I believe we are on the verge of a global transformation—a complete shift in the world order as we know it. We are on the brink of a species-level evolution.

We are in the century of the woman.

This book is one of many that are popping up everywhere helping girls and women to celebrate their bodies, their minds and their spirits. There is, I believe, an underground current—a claiming of space—where the world of the mother, the girl, the woman is coming to the fore. We may still possess magical healing powers for skinned knees and give great butter-fly kisses, but we are also passionate, wise, and *very* powerful. While I don't know the exact course this transformation will take, there is one thing of which I am absolutely certain:

Our children will be safe, nourished, and loved . . .

When mothers rule the world.

EPILOGUE

It's morning now as I write. I've traveled to the South Carolina coast to put some finishing touches on this book. The sun filters through the blinds and my cats have curled up in the block of light that rests on the floor.

I am always struck speechless by the peace I feel when I take time to be quiet, to sit in the stillness of the morning or the cool of the night. Most days I am wrapped up in activity from morning to night—a crazy pace that has me completely at my wit's end by bedtime.

As I sit now, in the quiet of the morning, I realize that I have a long way to go. I'm still caught in the crazy web of a culture gone haywire. I am still trying, many days, to live up to the cultural expectation that women can have it all, be everything to everybody. I realize that when I am most stressed I become a lazy, angry parent. I don't discipline my children. I don't appreciate them. I don't watch them while they sleep. When I am rushed, I don't take time to look at the world that lies on the path from my front door to my car. I am always running from one place to another. If I'm here, I should be there. If I'm there, I should be here.

Recently, my two kids and I moved into our first house. We got to the house an hour or two before the movers followed up with the bigger pieces of furniture. We brought in the smaller items and laid them on the floor of the living room.

We had never been in our own house with a yard and big trees. So the three of us sat on the front porch waiting for the movers. The summer day was brilliant and very hot. The shade from the sugar maple in the front yard cast a cool shadow on the bright green grass. Hank jumped off the porch, hopped down the steps, and lay down on the green carpet of our small but welcoming yard. Helen followed suit and I, too, joined them to feel the damp grass on my skin. We lay there for thirty minutes, watching the leaves of that maple tree dance in the wind. Cotton-candy clouds floated across the sky.

The three of us talked about our new house. I retold them the story of their births (they can listen to that story over and over) and we let the contrast of sun and shade wrap around our bodies like the sweet, colorful stripes of candy canes. Sometime during the thirty minutes, there was a period of two to three minutes of quiet. We listened to the wind. Hank didn't budge an inch. "Isn't this nice?" he said.

I didn't answer him. I didn't need to.

The moment was as nice as any moment will ever be.

Being a parent, a mentor, a child-supporter doesn't take time. It gives time. Time we may have let slip by being too busy, too angry, and too stressed in our rush-rush-*rush* world.

My children and the girls that I play with every day already know what they need to be calm, content little beings. They naturally love themselves, love others, and celebrate their child-strengths. They can sit still for minutes and examine the wonder of a fuzzy caterpillar as it inches its way across the sidewalk—or stare at the puffs of clouds as they float across the sky.

Sometime around middle school the world lowers the Girl Box down on our natural inclination to love ourselves, find joy in our bodies, and celebrate our strengths. My children, thankfully, are not at that stage yet. If I slow down long enough, sit still, breathe in the swirling wind, and look at the world through their eyes, I can see what they see. I can love myself and others unconditionally. I can celebrate the little girl I was and the woman I have become. I can let the clouds float by and feel the cool green grass on my skin.

And I can know without question that this life is very nice indeed.

Acknowledgments

I would like to thank:

First, my Higher Power. It lives in me, you, the flowers that bloom in winter, and the rain that falls in summer.

James B. for teaching me that I will be all right on my own.

Hank B. for letting me still hold him even though he is a big boy.

Helen B. for letting me know that I dress funny and it doesn't matter.

Frank B. for showing me that leaders can be skinny, five-foot-four, and disinterested in politics.

Randy W. for sharing the love of his daughter.

Jenny B., my literary agent, for believing in this project and being the only Southern girl I know who can say *fabulous* like a true New Yorker.

Allison Dickens, my editor at Ballantine. Allison was and is *always* encouraging, enthusiastic, and, above all, my best advocate. Thank you so much, Allison. You definitely "get it"!

Russ P. for teaching me the power of my personality.

David Q. for helping me prioritize the most important things in my life.

Karen R. for walking me through the steps and loving me unconditionally.

Elaine M. for your depth of commitment to a spiritual life and your pulling me in that direction.

Sidney P. for teaching me to let go.

Patti M. for believing in me.

Kathi T. for being the most vulnerable person I know and giving me permission to be likewise.

Bryan C. for helping me see the writer that hides in my soul.

All the little girls who have ever been in Girls on the Run—you are God's greatest gift.

All of the women (and men) who have helped nurture the Girls on the Run program. We can do this!

Richard W., for crying at my stories, letting me be my real self, and talking with me into the "black liquid of night."

Helen N., my sister, for taking care of me when no one else would. Or could.

Emily W. for being my sister and a teacher in the ways of spirituality.

David K., Emily's new husband, for giving me hope.

Henry W., my brother, for calling it like you see it, even when it hurts.

Hank W., my father, who planted in me the sincere desire to leave the world a better place than I entered it.

And, most important, my mother, Mary Wilmer, who lived the life I yearn to live. Her daily contact with God, her kindness, her love of the earth and its creatures, her momentous impact on the lives of all she came into contact with, and her unconditional love and undying belief that I would be all right. I thank you for your life and for your death, because through your dying I am called to practice what I preach—living a life of forgiveness of myself and others—and have been forced to rely totally and completely on my relationship with my Higher Power. Mom, I'm doing okay. Helen, Hank, and I miss you so much. We love you.

© Brian Gomsak

ABOUT THE AUTHOR

MOLLY BARKER, M.S.W., a four-time Hawaii Ironman triathlete, founded GOTR® in Charlotte, North Carolina, in 1996. Molly began running at the age of fifteen—an age when she found herself stuck in the Girl Box, when only girls who were a certain size with a certain beauty were popular. Molly kept running and years later, on July 7, 1993, she took off on a sunset run and found the inspiration that grew into Girls on the Run®. Using her background in counseling and teaching and her personal recovery from alcoholism, along with research on adolescent issues, she developed the earliest version of the curriculum with the help of thirteen intrepid girls at Charlotte Country Day School. The program grew and today Molly oversees more than 20,000 girls who participate in GOTR programs across the country. In 1998, *Runner's World,* a national running magazine, awarded Molly its Golden Shoe Award for contributions to the community through running. Her favorite times remain the ones she spends with her own daughter and her son at their home in Charlotte, North Carolina.